Translation
Ivor Neil Coward

Photographic credits
Archivio della Soprintendenza
per i Beni Artistici
e Storici di Venezia
Archivio Electa
Foto Böhm, Venezia

Reprint 2000

Soprintendenza per i Beni Artistici e Storici di Venezia

The Accademia Galleries in Venice

edited by
Giovanna Nepi Scirè

Electa

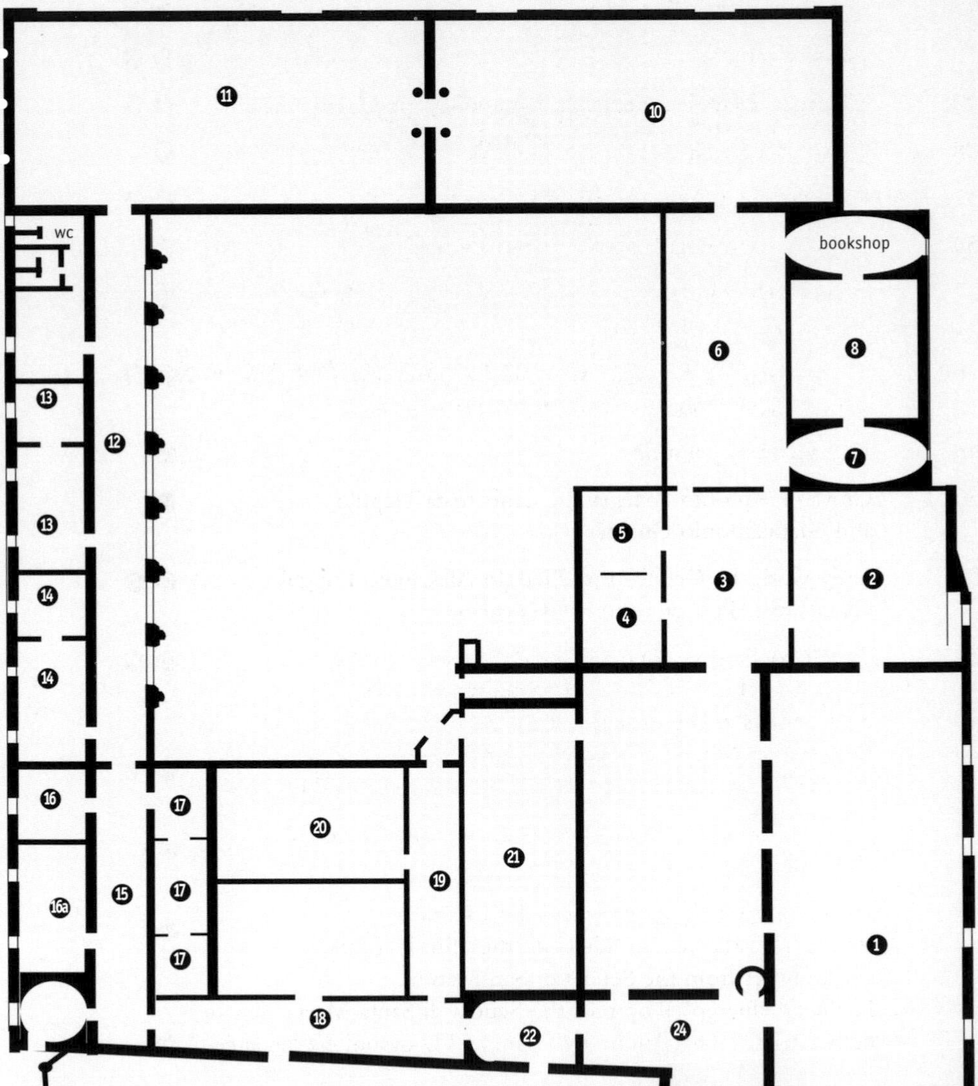

11
10
wc
bookshop
6
8
7
13
12
13
5
3
2
4
14
14
16
17
20
21
19
16a
15
17
17
1
18
22
24
23

The Accademia Galleries

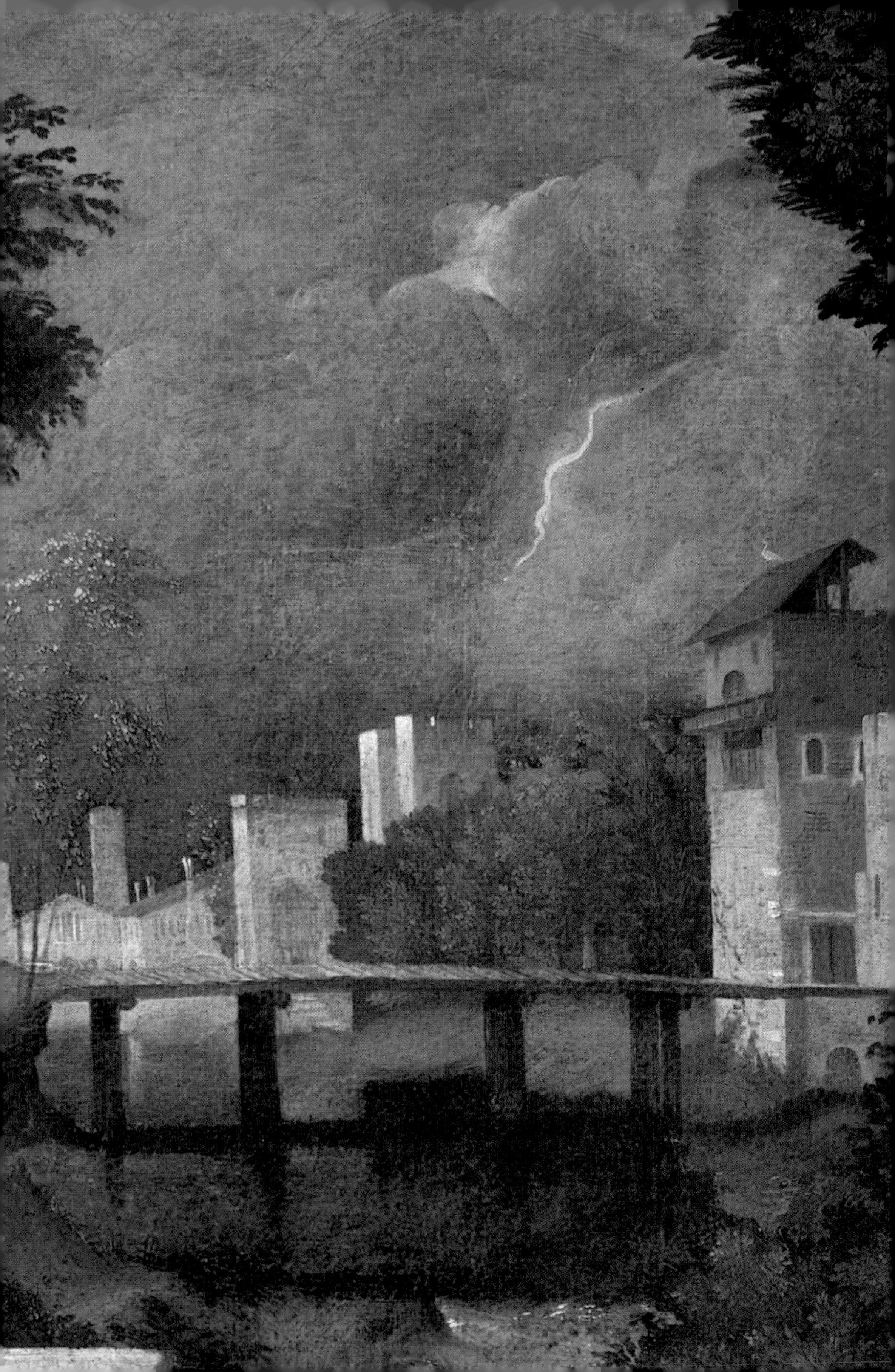

The Accademia Galleries

Giovanna Nepi Scirè

In the early 1800's, the Galleries of the Accademia – containing the most important collection of 14th - to 18th-Century Venetian painting – along with the Brera Picture Gallery and Bologna Accademia, became a museum with very political origins, closely connected to the local events that, in those years, had reduced Venice to little more than a prize passed around among the great European powers.

With the annexation under the Napoleonic Kingdom of Italy after the treaty of Presburg in 1805, all the public palazzi and religious buildings were closed, and others were even destroyed. The artwork that surfaced from these events and which was somehow not sold or lost, found protection in the new Galleries. Originally, however, the Galleries' purpose was largely as an instructional tool, as is shown in the decree of September 1, 1803, extended on February 12, 1807 also to Venice, which established that – alongside an academy of fine arts divided into various faculties – there would be a gallery for the "benefit of those who practise painting".

The Venetian Academy of Fine Arts was also forced to relocate from the Fonteghetto della Farina (small wheat warehouse) to a group of buildings which included the convent of the Lateran Canons, designed by Andrea Palladio in 1561, the Church of La Carità, reconstructed by Bartolomeo Bon between 1441 and 1452, and the Scuola della Carità, the first of the great Venetian schools, founded in 1260. Thus there was also the problem of how to incorporate the works of art into structures whose original purpose was entirely different, and which were not connected to one another in any way.

The restructuring project was led by Giannantonio Selva and lasted until 1811. It was necessary to completely gut the church which, once the furnishings and altars were removed, was then divided horizontally and vertically to create five large rooms on the lower floor for the school and two on the upper floor to serve as exhibition rooms. These spaces were created after walling over the Gothic windows, with illumination coming from above. The buildings were connected by opening a passageway on the first floor at the back wall of the Albergo Room, and constructing a short stairway which led through a foyer to the other rooms.

The rooms of the Scuola della Carità were largely left the same: the wooden ceiling from the late 15th Century is still in the Albergo Room (room 24), as are the triptych by Antonio Vivarini and Giovanni d'Alemagna dated at 1446, and Titian's *Presentation* which dates from August 31, 1534 to March 6, 1539. Also intact – aside from the fact that the altar was removed – is the great old Assembly hall (room 1), where the sumptuous ceiling remains on display with its deep blue and gold lacunars, carved by Marco Cozzi from 1461 to 1484. The five central high-reliefs were removed

Giorgione, La Tempesta, *detail*

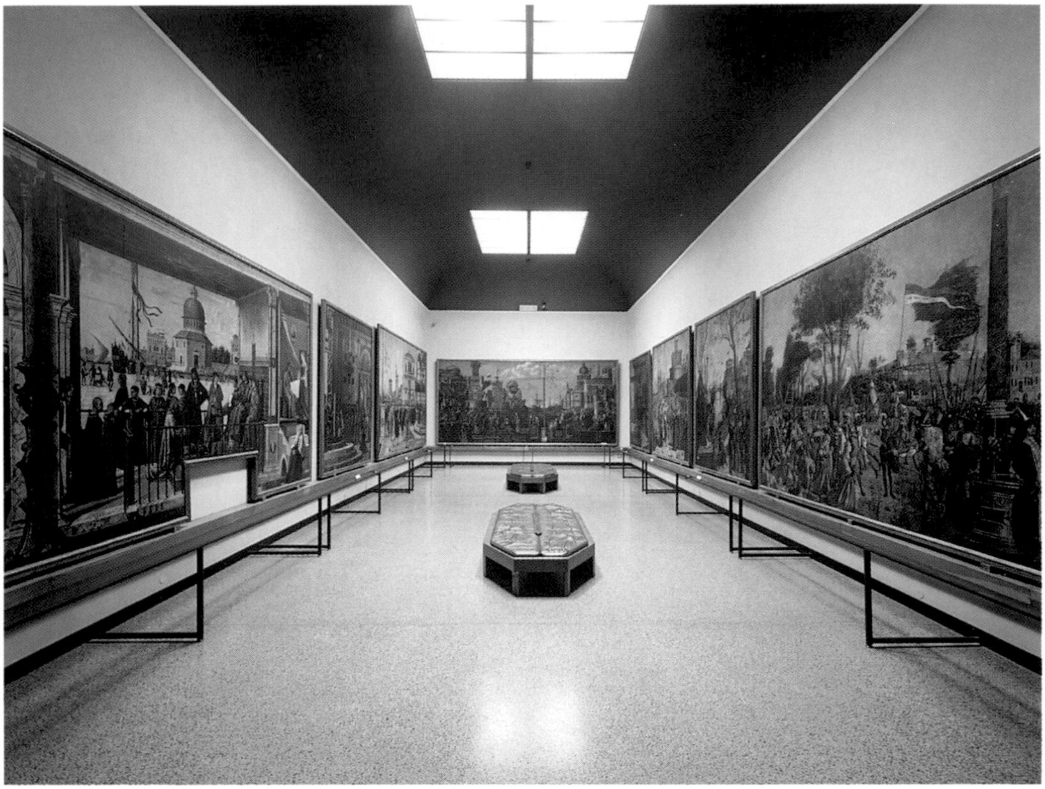

Room 21
(Vittore Carpaccio's "Saint Ursula cycle")

around 1814, and were replaced with four *Prophets* by Domenico Campagnola or Stefano dell'Arzere, from the Scuola della Madonna del Parto in Padua, and a *Holy Father* traditionally attributed to Alvise Vivarini, but more likely by Pier Maria Pennacchi, once in the Venetian chapel of San Girolamo. It was decidedly more difficult to reconfigure the Palladian convent, however, especially since its integrity had already been somewhat compromised by a fire in 1630. Selva approached it with caution: the arcades of the Ionic loggia were closed, leaving some half-moons for lighting and to provide greater exhibition surface; the windows on the Sant'Agnese canal were raised, and the cells on the last floor were modified to create the engraving school and housing for the professors.
On August 10, 1817, the gallery was opened to the public for a short time, with a great number of visitors.
The first items to be included in the collection were a small number of artists' works, donations and trial works by the members of the Academy which were brought over from the old Academy Abbot Farsetti, some of the remaining paintings from the Scuola della Carità, and collection of plasters acquired from the Austrian government in 1805. Other important works were sent to the Brera Gallery in Milan, but luckily some paintings were added that France had returned, among which Paolo Veronese's famous *Christ in the House of Levi*. Others were removed from Venetian churches, such as that of San Giobbe, and placed in the Accademia Galleries as a precautionary measure, and yet other paintings were added from the first private contributions to the gallery. Some acquisitions – which were significant although few when compared with the enormous availa-

bility on the market – further enriched the patrimony. This notwithstanding, the collection continued to favour and protect Venetian painting – as it does now – and so was not particularly suitable for a well-rounded artistic education. During the 1800's, much effort was made to balance out this situation until the end of the Century, when interest in the didactic aspect had all but vanished and with it the desire to expand the breadth of the gallery's collection.

Nonetheless, the Accademia anticipated the intentions of the Brera Gallery and through Abbot Celotti acquired Giuseppe Bossi's prestigious drawing collection, which boasted more than three thousand pieces and included – in addition to folios by Leonardo da Vinci and the famous *Vitruvian Man* – drawings from the Bolognese, Roman, Tuscan, Ligurian and Lombard schools, not to mention the German, French and Flemish schools that provided a certain uniformity to the collection of paintings.

As the number of art works increased, so too did the exhibition spaces become (and so will they always be) wholly insufficient and overcrowded. The enlarged floor designed by Selva, who died in 1819, was constructed under the supervision of Francesco Lazzari, and provided for two large halls to the left of the Palladian convent (rooms 11 and 70). In 1828 both these halls were built, and the first one was opened; the second was not completed until 1834. In 1829 Lazzari completely remodelled the convent: in the courtyard he destroyed the arches inspired by Palladian perspective and left intact by Selva, and expanded the ends with two intercolumniations. He reopened the curtained sections of the Ionic arches,

Rooms 4 and 5 (Giovanni Bellini, Andrea Mantegna, Piero della Francesca, Jacopo Bellini, Cosmè Tura, Hans Memling and Giorgione)

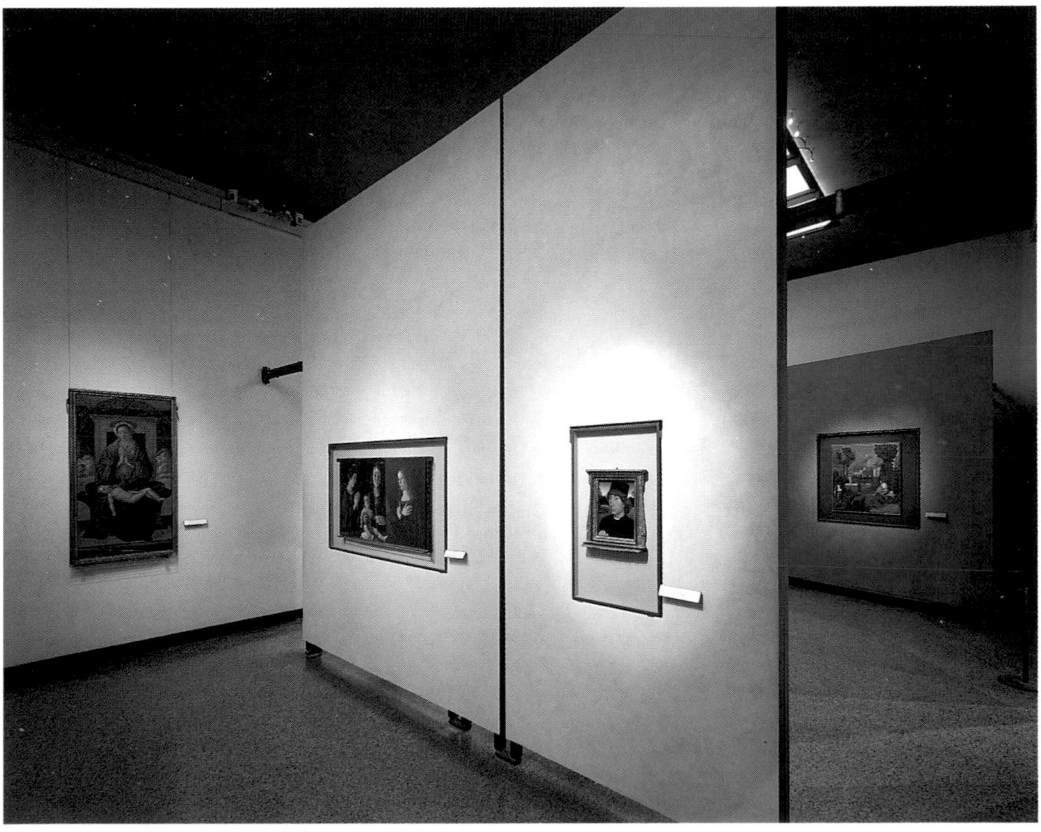

while at a later time both these and the Doric arches were fitted with large windows. In 1830 the façade was also modified: the emblems of La Carità were replaced with those of the Accademia, windows were opened in the niches, and a sculpture – now located at the Public Gardens – by Antonio Giacarelli depicting Minerva seated upon the Adriatic lion, was placed at the top. Initially, the annexation to the Kingdom of Italy did not bring about large-scale changes, but from 1870 the school gradually became separate from the Accademia Galleries. This took place through various stages, including decrees in 1878 and 1879. The collection, entrusted to the supervision of the president of the Accademia, was officially delivered to him on January 15, 1881, while on March 13, 1882, definitive independence was sanctioned for both the school and the Accademia Galleries.

In 1895 the galleries were radically reconfigured by the director, Giulio Cantalamessa. By eliminating works by artists of the 1800's and consolidating the few paintings from other Italian and foreign schools, he tried for the first time to establish a chronological order. The unitary cycles from the 15th Century schools of San Giovanni Evangelista and Sant'Orsola – which before had been spread out – were regrouped into two rooms of the church. 16th Century Veneto paintings were placed in the corridors. He also removed the bronzes, which were later brought together again in the Franchetti Gallery at Ca' d'Oro. Cantalamessa thus established what has remained the primary focus of the Accademia: a collection of Veneto painting from the 14th to the 18th Centuries.

Cantalamessa was succeeded by Gino Fogolari in 1905, and little was done to the Accademia itself, although the collection of drawings and paintings continued to expand under his long direction. After World War I, Fogolari lobbied for important pieces of art which had originally belonged to Venice to be returned from Austria. During the war, the most important paintings had been kept in Florence. From 1921 to 1923, as these pieces were being returned, the museum was again remodelled. The Accademia lost Titian's *Assumption*, which was returned to the Church of the Frari. The two rooms dedicated to the canvases of the *Ursula* cycle and the *Cross* cycle were eliminated, creating one large space with apses and restoring the truss ceiling and the Gothic windows on the side walls.

As under the direction of Cantalamessa, once again the works from the 19th Century were removed and placed in storage at Ca' Pesaro; a similar fate lay in store for the paintings from foreign schools, which were moved to the Franchetti Gallery. The immediate need to implement more modern criteria for the museum reached its culmination during the 1940's, and especially when direction of the Accademia passed to Vittorio Moschini in 1941. Moschini worked with Carlo Scarpa even while World War II was underway to formulate a more articulate restructuring. The urgency to rebuild other Italian museums made it impossible to carry out the vast transformations that they had planned, but nonetheless a renovation project was begun which marked the end of a museum model that had remained unchanged since the turn of the Century.

Recently a gallery was opened in the long wing of the Palladian hall on the second floor, increasing public access to more than eighty masterpieces of the collection. Even more recently much maintenance work has been carried out on the building itself, with a revision of all the fittings and an intense restoration effort on the paintings themselves.

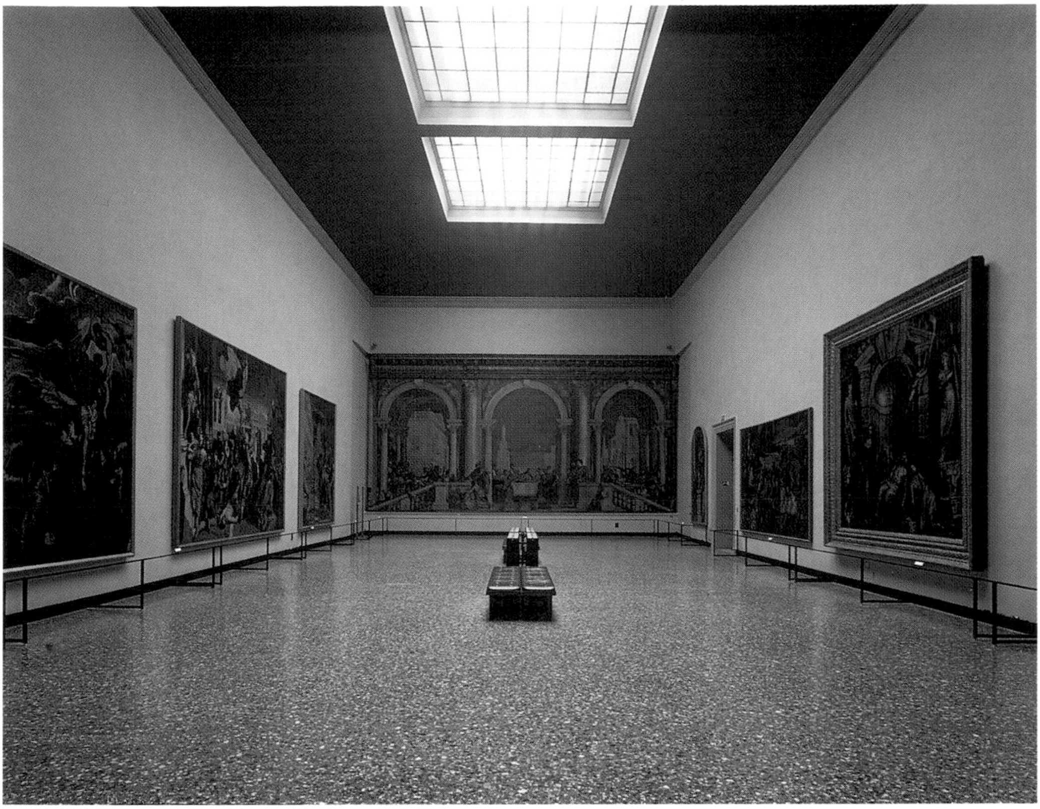

Room 10
(Titian, Paolo Veronese
and Jacopo Tintoretto)

Essential Bibliography

B. Berenson, *Pittura italiana del Rinascimento. La scuola Veneta*, 2 vols., Londra-Firenze 1958.

Hope Charles, *A New Document about Titian's Pietà* in *Sight & Insight: Essays on Art and Culture in Honour of E.H. Gombrich at 85*, ed. John Onlans, pp. 153-67. London, 1994.

P. Humfrey, *The Altarpiece in Renaissance Venice*, New Haven-London 1993.

M. Lucco, *La Pittura a Venezia nel primo Cinquecento* and S. Mason Rinaldi, *La Pittura a Venezia nel secondo Cinquecento* in *La Pittura in Italia. Il Cinquecento*, 2 vols., Milano 1988.

S. Moschini Marconi, *Gallerie dell'Accademia di Venezia. Opere d'arte dei secoli XIV e XV*, Roma 1955.

Id., *Gallerie dell'Accademia di Venezia. Opere d'arte del secolo XVI*, Roma 1962.

Id., *Gallerie dell'Accademia di Venezia. Opere d'arte dei secoli XVII, XVIII, XIX*, Roma 1970.

G. Nepi Scirè, *I capolavori dell'arte veneziana. Le Gallerie dell'Accademia*, Venezia 1991.

G. Nepi Scirè-F. Valcanover, *Gallerie dell'Accademia di Venezia*, Milano 1985.

R. Pallucchini, *Pittura del Trecento*, Roma 1964.

Id., *La pittura veneziana del Seicento*, 2 vols., Milano 1981.

Id., *La pittura nel Veneto. Il Settecento*, 2 vols., Milano 1994.

Various Authors, *La pittura nel Veneto. Il Trecento*, Milano 1992.

Various Authors, *La pittura nel Veneto. Il Quattrocento*, Milano 1990.

Various Authors, *La pittura nel Veneto. Il Cinquecento*, 3 vols., Milano 1996-1999.

F. Zeri (ed.), *La pittura in Italia. Il Quattrocento*, 2 vols., Milano 1987.

The Primitives

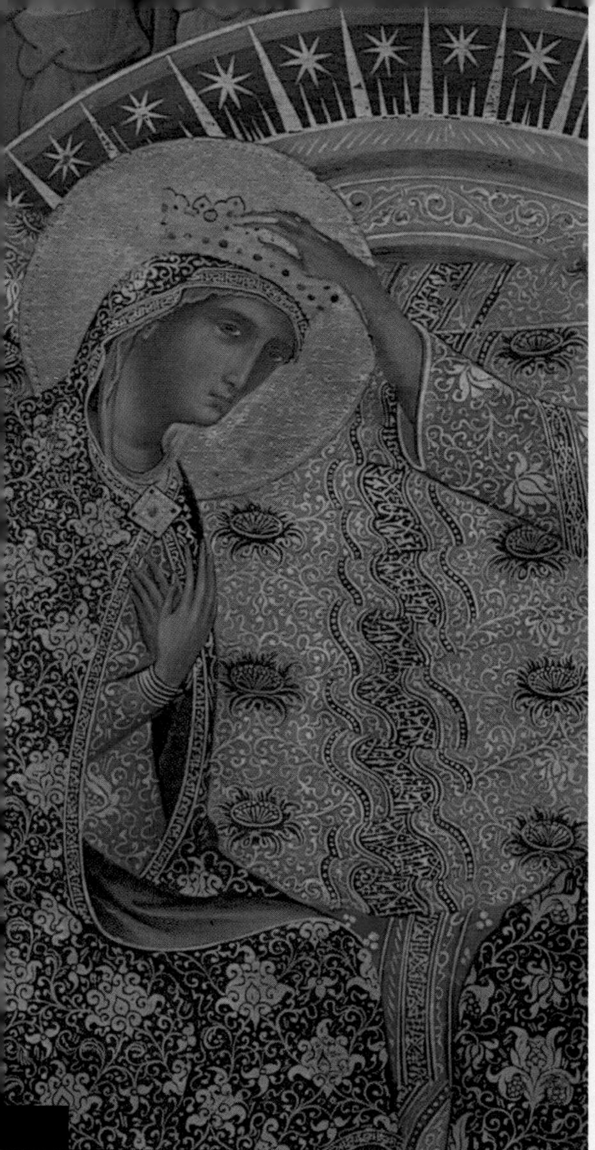

This was the room in which the chapter of the great Scuola di Santa Maria della Carità met, the oldest of the six great schools of Venice. These schools were powerful secular guilds for devotion and assistance to the poor. The ceiling, constructed between 1461 and 1484 by Marco Cozzi of Vicenza, is made up of square lacunars with leaf decorations on the side and heads of angels with eight wings, each with different facial characteristics. The blue background and the original colours of the figures have resurfaced from the gilt decoration made in the 1700's, thanks to a long restoration project completed in 1992. The paintings in the compartments, however, do not belong to the original decoration: at the centre there is the *Holy father*, probably the work of Pier Maria Pennacchi (1464–1514/1515), while at the corners there are the four Prophets attributed to Domenico Campagnola or Stefano dell'Arzere (documents dating from 1540 to 1575). The polychrome marble paving dates to the remodelling of the 1700's. The rooms underwent other modifications at the beginning of the 1800's, when the entire complex of buildings became the Accademia: the back altar was removed, the windows were walled over to increase exhibition space and the original paintings were replaced with works which were to form the new gallery (including Titian's *Assumption*, now in the Church of the Frari). The present-day configuration of the room is the work of Carlo Scarpa, which he began in 1950. He recovered the openings of the windows, restored the fragments of the late fourteenth-century pictorial mural decoration and placed the gold-ground panels on wooden partitions with iron bases still supporting them today. In this room are displayed works by Jacobello del Fiore, Paolo Veneziano, Lorenzo Veneziano, Giovanni da Bologna, Jacobello Alberegno, Catarino, Michele Giambono, Stefano "Plebanus" di Sant'Agnese, Antonio Vivarini, Nicolò di Pietro, Jacopo Moranzone, the Veneto-Byzantine school of the 14th and 15th Centuries, the Venetian school of the second half of the 14th Century,
the Veneto school of the end of the 14th Century, and the Rimini school.

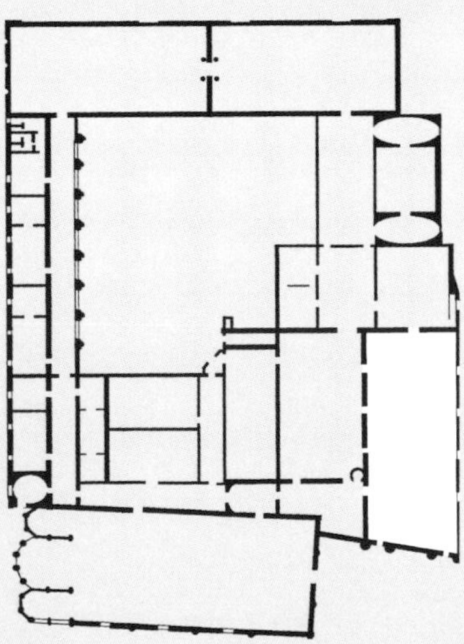

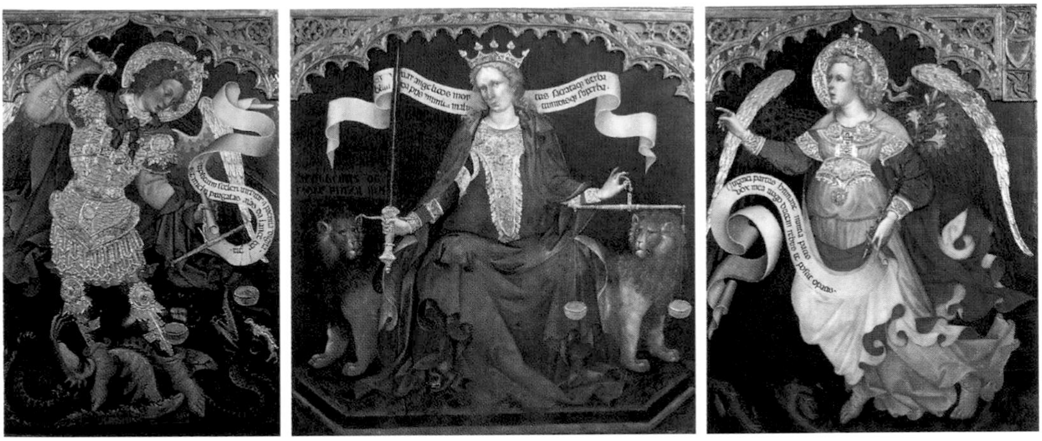

Jacobello del Fiore
records in Venice
from 1400 to 1439

Justice and the Archangels Triptych

Acquisition: 1884 (cat. 15)
Latest restoration: 1997
At the centre, the allegory of Justice. To the left, Saint Michael slaying the dragon – a symbol of Satan. To the right, the arch-angel Gabriel. In the painting, which was probably completed in 1421 for the Ducal Palace, Justice is clearly identified with Venice, and Peace with the Virgin Mary.

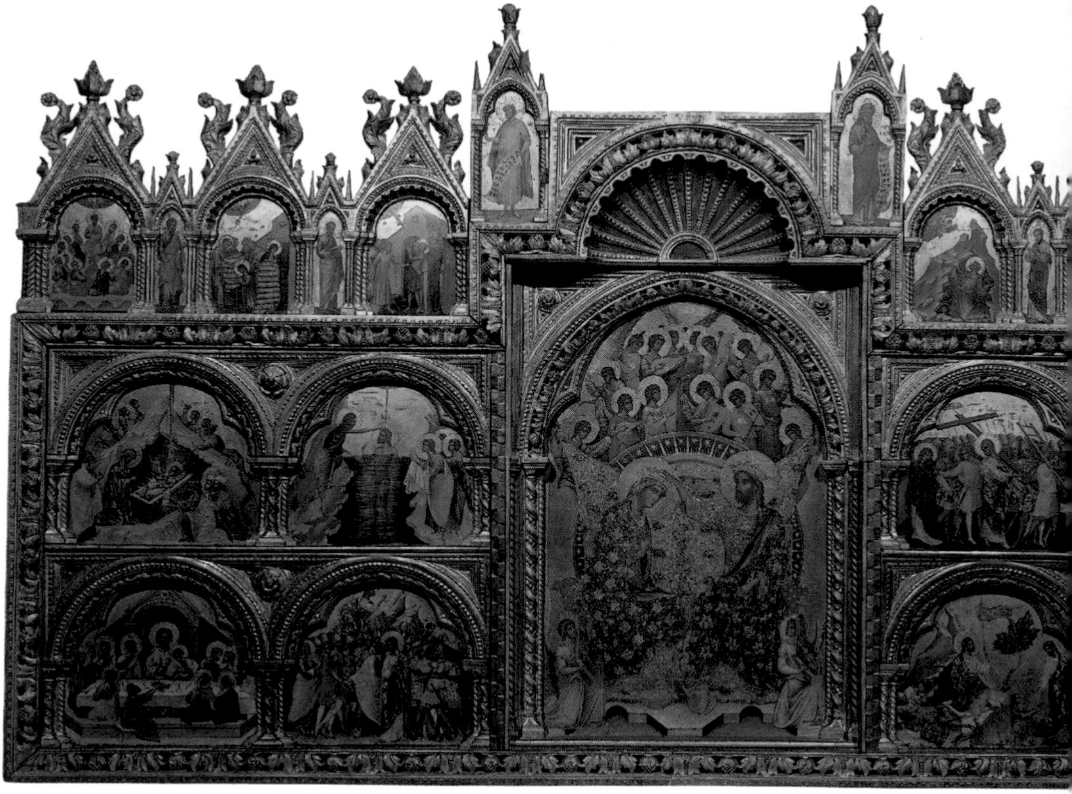

1

Michele Giambono
records from 1420
to 1462

Saint James and Saints

Acquisition: 1812 (cat. 3)
Latest restoration: 1979

Dated at around 1450, the polyptych is believed to come from the church of San Giacomo on the island of Giudecca. The elegant play of the lines – especially evident in the figure of Saint Michael – expresses the decorative taste typical of the late-Gothic style of painting which Giambono practised in Venice.

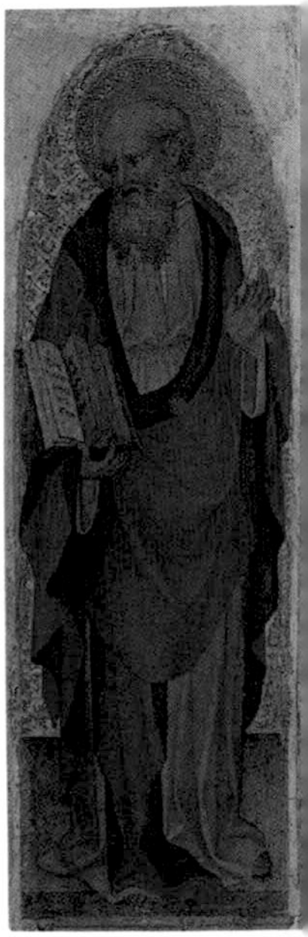

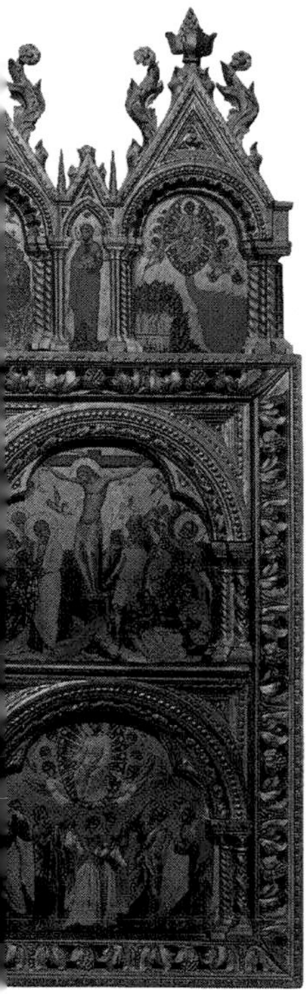

Paolo Veneziano
active from 1333 to 1358
died before 1362

Acquisition: 1812, 1950 for the central panel (cat. 21)
Latest restoration: 1951

At the centre, the Coronation of the Virgin. At the sides, the stories of Christ. On the upper crowing, at left: the Pentecost, Saint Matthew, the veil-taking ceremony of Saint Claire, Saint John, Saint Francis gives back his clothes to his father; on the right the stigmate of Saint Francis, Saint Mark, the death of Saint Francis, Saint Luke, Christ the judge. At the centre: the two prophets Isaiah and Daniel. Dating to around 1350, this work came from the Church of Santa Chiara.

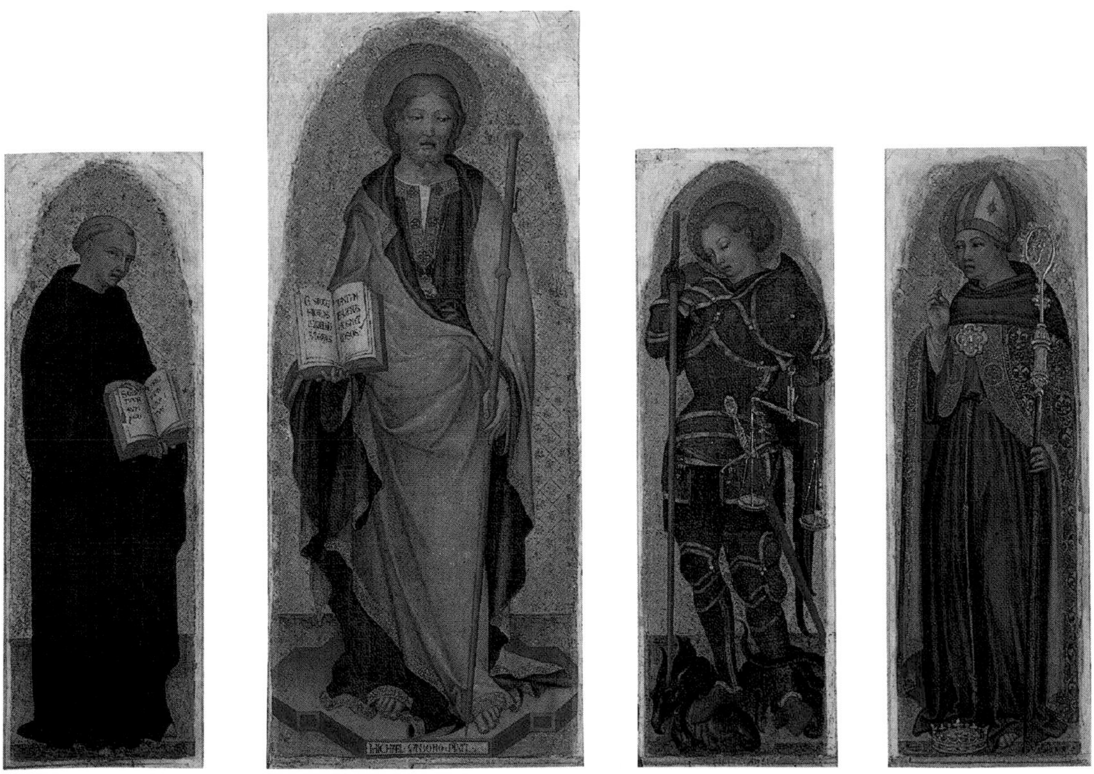

Nicolò di Pietro
records from 1356
to 1372

Madonna with Child

Acquisition: 1856 (cat. 19)
Latest restoration: 1949

Under the footboard of the throne the date 1394, the name of the commissioner – kneeling to the left – and the signature of the artist and his address at the foot of the ponte del Paradiso. In this first known and dated work of Nicolò di Pietro, there are many clear references to the Bolognese figurative style.

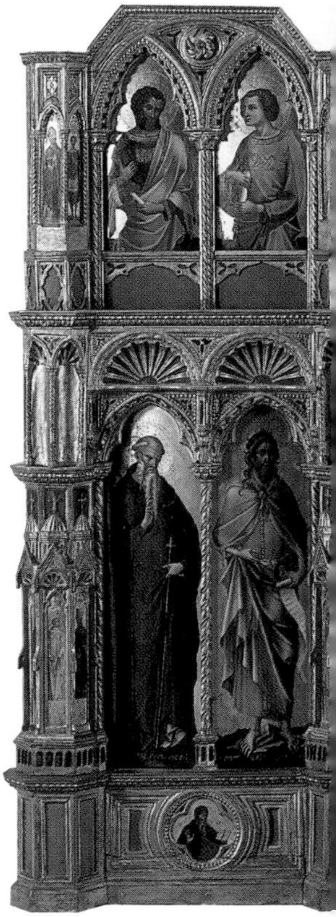

1

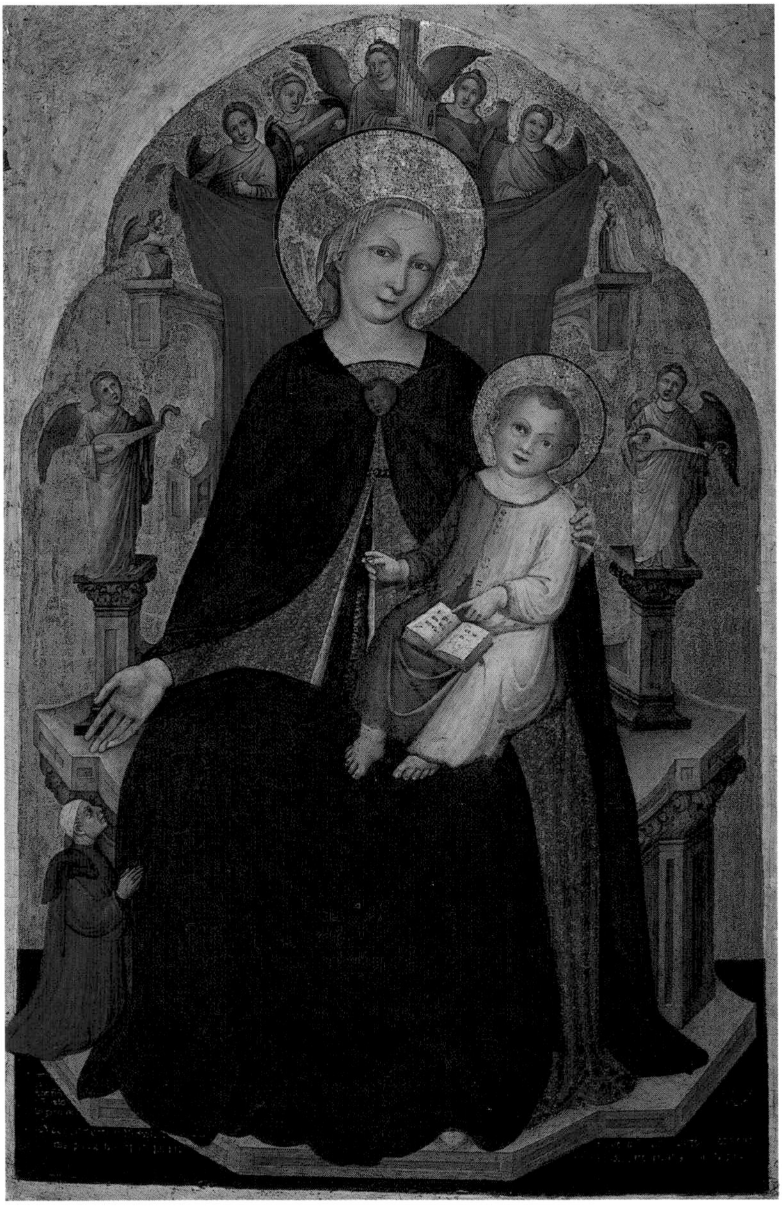

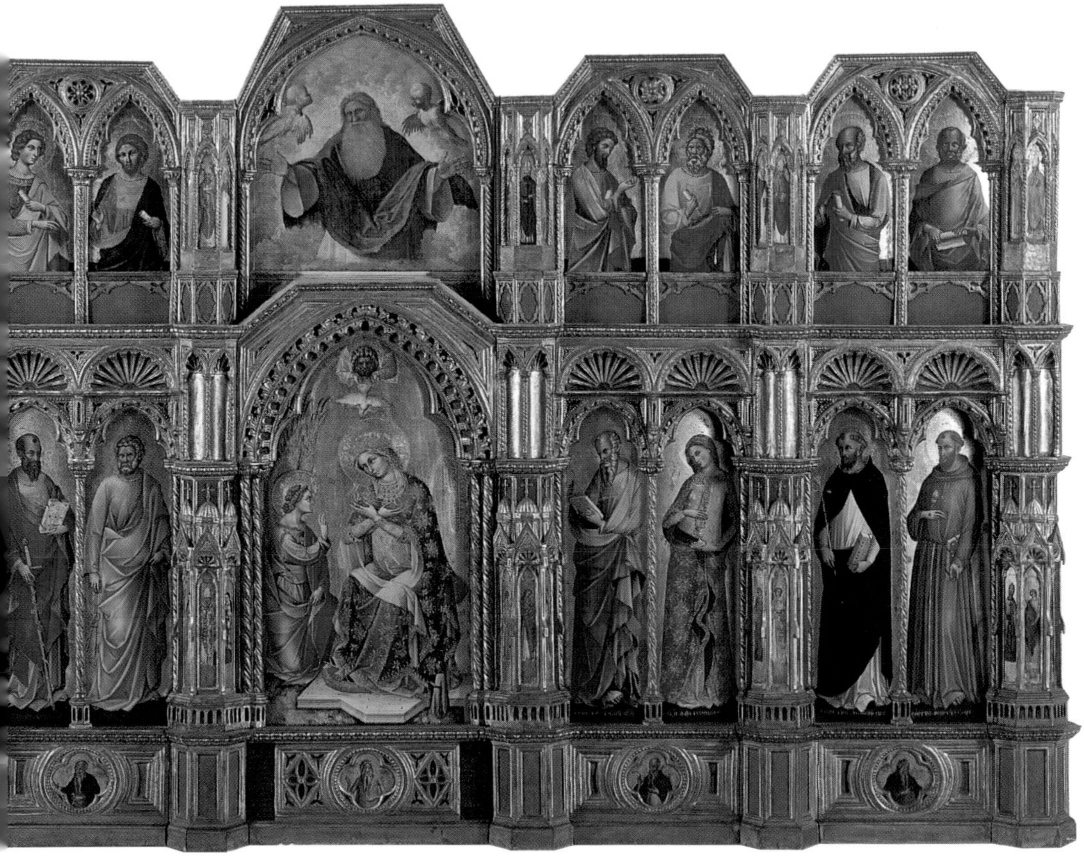

1

Lorenzo Veneziano
records from 1356
to 1372

Annunciation
(Lion Polyptych)

Acquisition: 1812 (cat. 10)
Latest restoration: 1997

At left, the saints Anthony (Abbot), John the Baptist, Paul and Peter. At right, saints John the Evangelist, Magdalene, Dominic and Francis.
On the upper order, the Holy Father giving his blessing among eight Prophets. Below, on the predella, are the hermit saints Saba, Macarius, Paul, Hilary and Theodore. The upper panel in the centre is a replacement of the original, which was lost, and is possibly the work of Benedetto Diana.

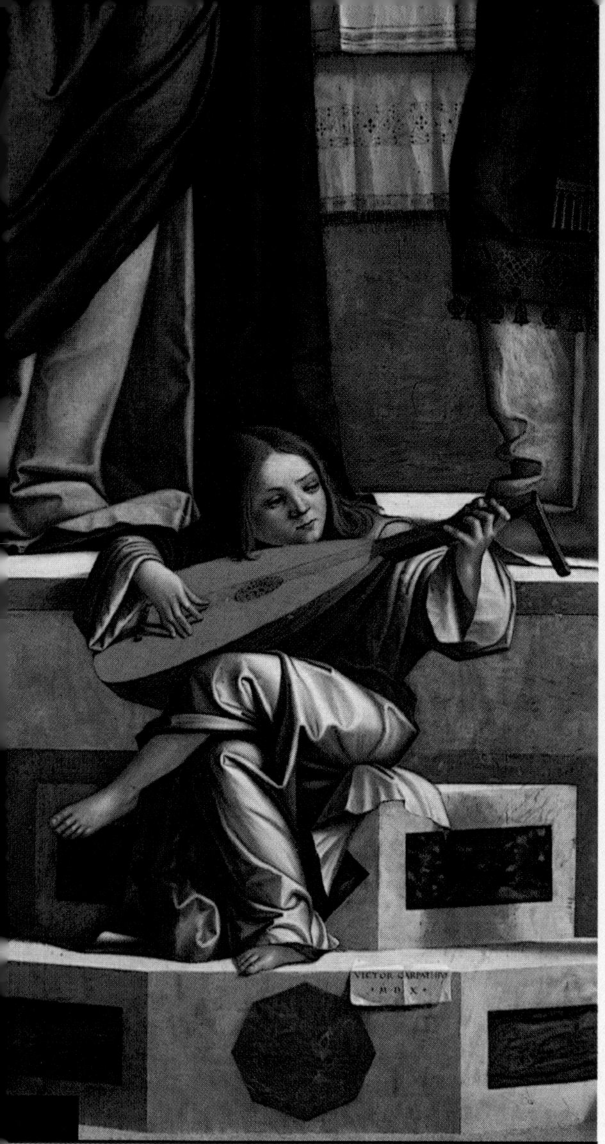

The Great 15th-Century Altarpieces, and Giovanni Bellini

Room 2. This room was constructed between 1886 and 1895 to house Titian's *Assumption* and other large altarpieces. After the *Assumption* was returned to the Church of the Frari in 1919, the room appeared rather out of balance. To restore the room's harmony, in 1951 Carlo Scarpa replaced the decorated ceiling with a dark green plaster, replaced the polychrome marble paving with a dark grey Venetian style "terrazzo", masked the entrance by a large masonry panel and created a new stairway to room 3.
In this room are shown works by Vittore Carpaccio, Marco Basaiti, Giovanni Bellini and Giambattista Cima da Conegliano.

Room 3. In this room are shown paintings by Sebastiano Luciani (del Piombo), Giambattista Cima da Conegliano, Giovanni Bellini and Giorgione.

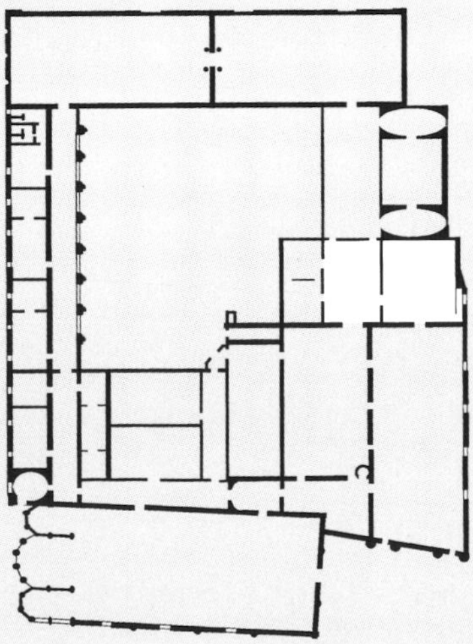

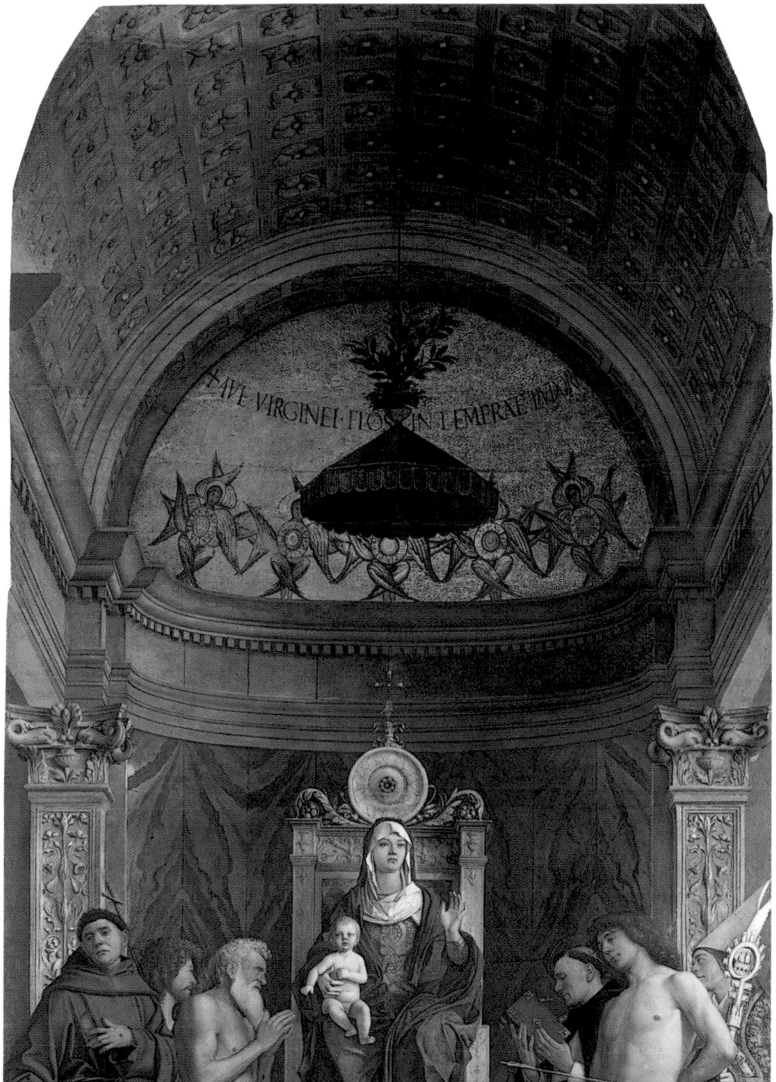

Giovanni Bellini
(Venice 1434/39-1516)

Madonna on the throne with child, with Saints Francis, John the Baptist, Job, Dominic, Sebastian, Ludovic and angels, known as *the San Giobbe altarpiece.*

Panel, 471 cm × 292 cm
(cat. 38)
Acquisition: 1815
Latest restoration: 1994-95

Originally in the Church of San Giobbe, on the altar of the title saint, which was second to the right. The great panel is shortened by 50 cm at the top. The presence of apotropaic saint Sebastian indicates that the altarpiece must have been made at the time of one of the plagues, probably that of 1478.

Vittore Carpaccio
(c. 1460-1526)

Presentation of Christ in the Temple

Panel, 420 cm × 231 cm
(cat. 44)
Acquisition: 1815
Latest restoration: 1995

Signed and dated 1510, the altarpiece was originally in the Church of San Giobbe in the third altar to the right. Jesus' presentation in the Temple – forty days after his birth – occurs in a space in the shape of an apse, whereas the figures are all composed in a pyramid.

2

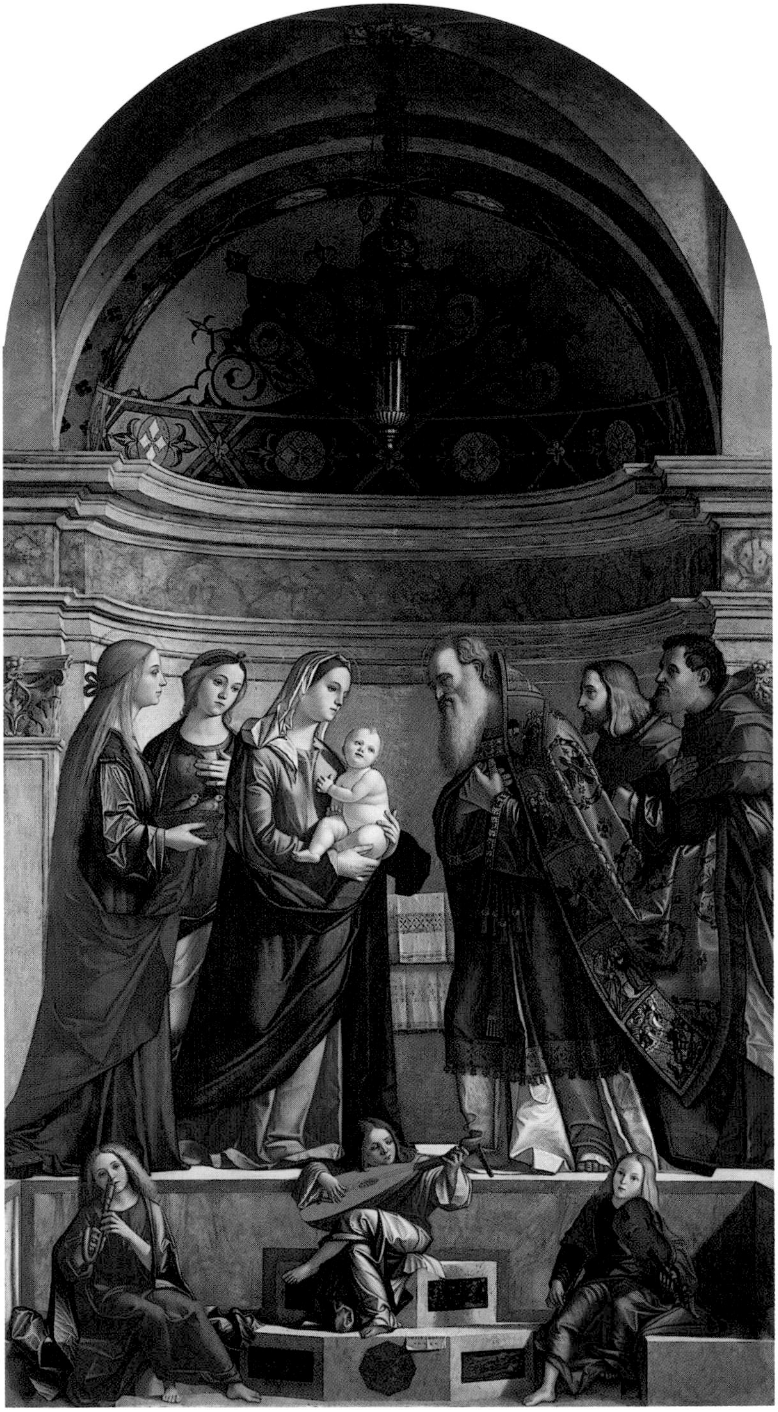

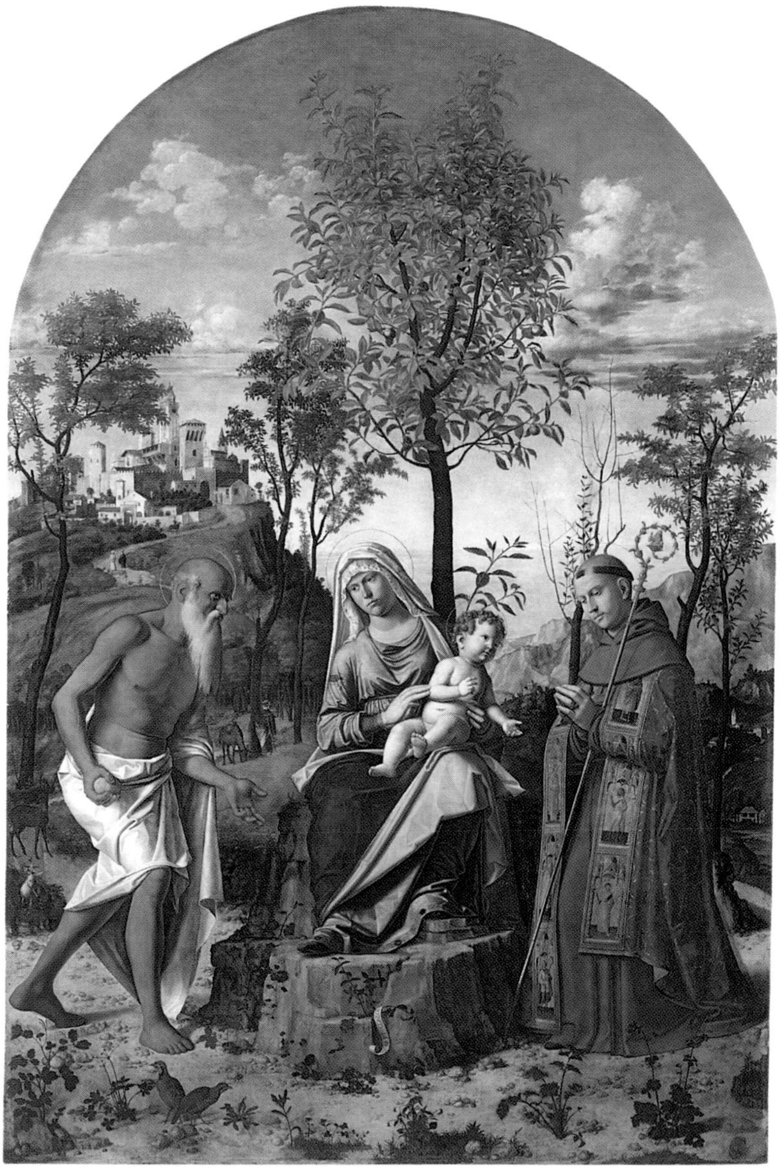

Giambattista Cima da Conegliano
(Conegliano1459-1517)

Madonna of the Orange Tree

Panel, 211 cm × 139 cm
(cat. 815)
Acquisition: 1919, returned from Austria
Latest restoration: 1995

This signed altarpiece was originally to the right of the main altar in the church of Santa Chiara on Murano. The theme is a variation on the Flight in Egypt, as is alluded to with saint Joseph and the ass in the background.

2

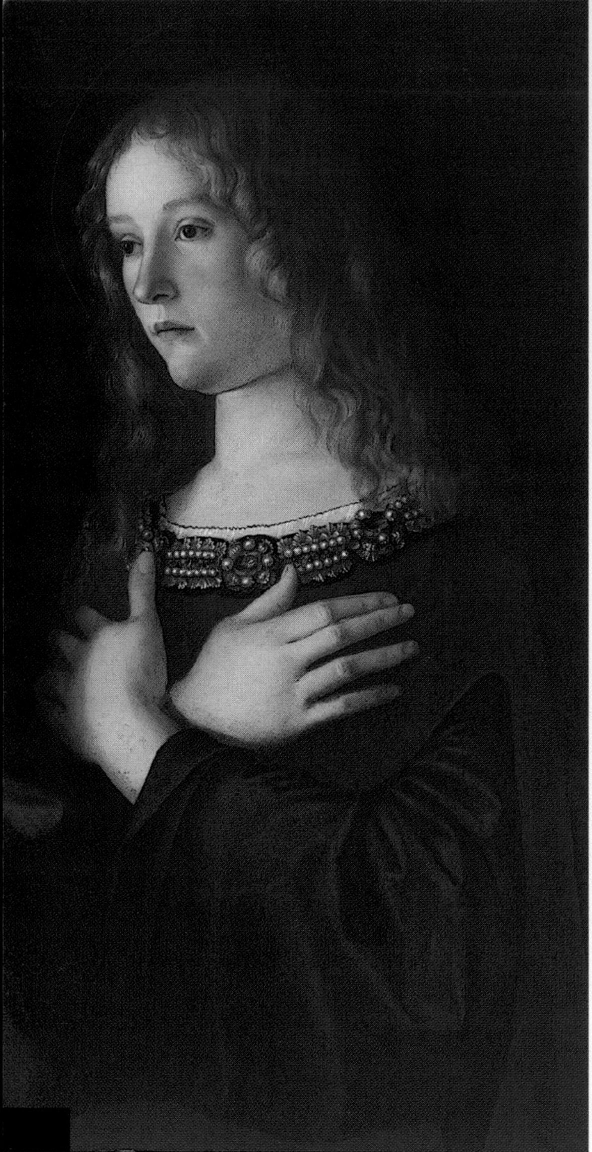

Mantegna, Piero della Francesca, Cosmè Tura and Giorgione

Carlo Scarpa redesigned these two rooms in 1955, walling over their windows and making them into one open space divided at the centre by a panel placed in correspondence with the two skylights that formerly occupied that spot. Works were shown using only original frames or frames of the same era; paintings which lacked a frame were inserted into wooden panels lined with material. For Giorgione's *Tempesta* a brown velvet was used.

Room 4. Works by Giovanni Bellini, Andrea Mantegna, Piero della Francesca, Jacopo Bellini, Cosmè Tura and Hans Memling.

Room 5. Works by Giovanni Bellini and Giorgione.

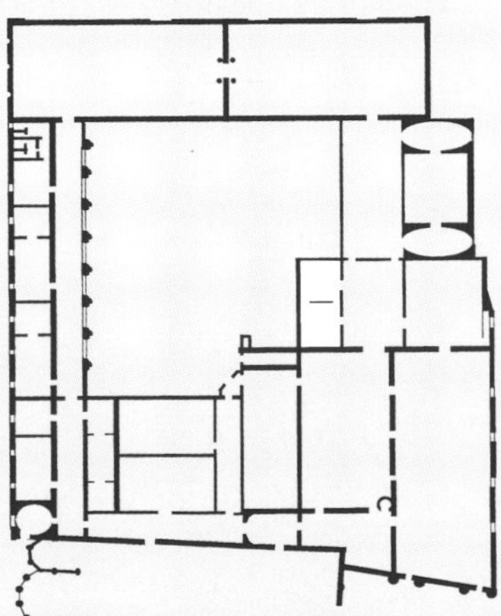

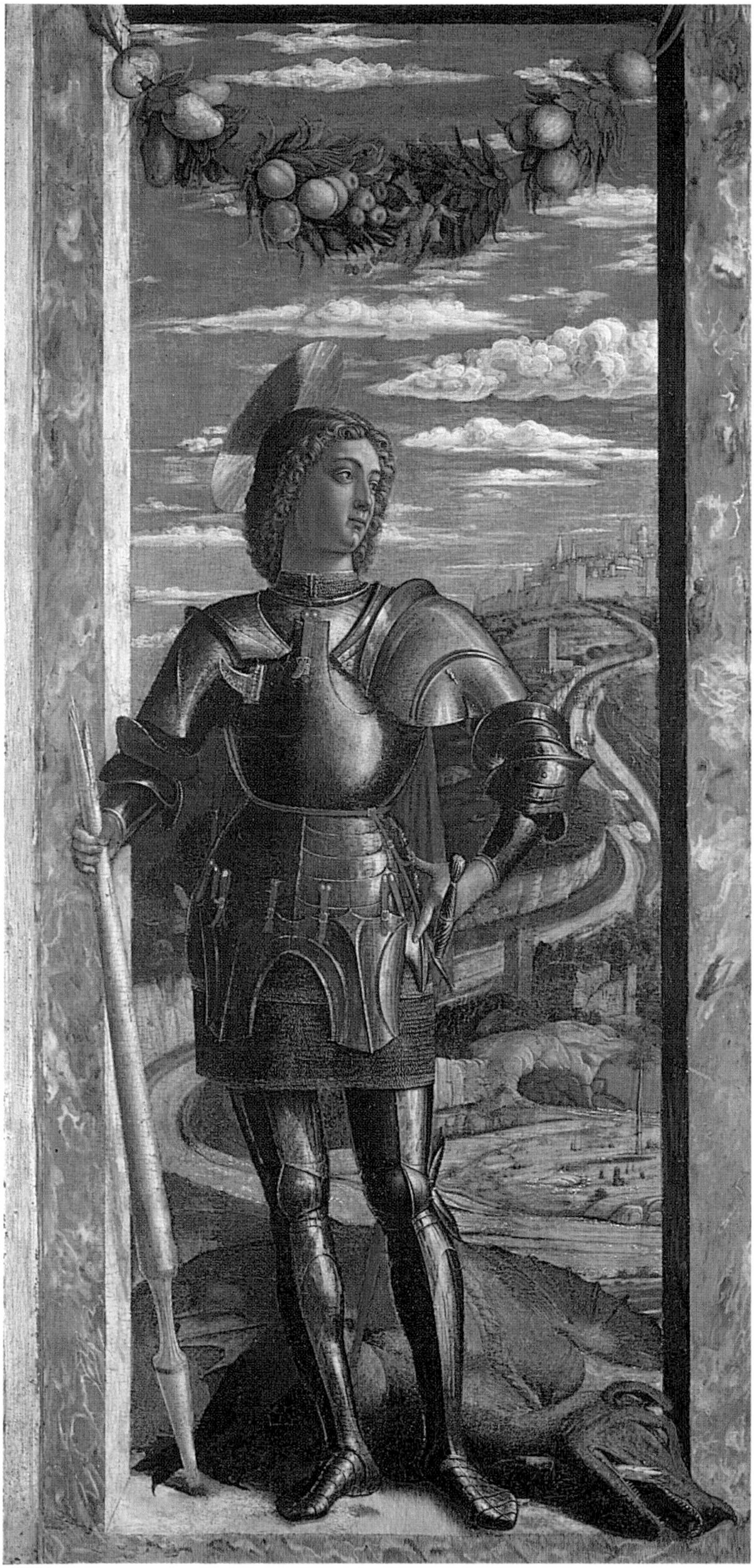

Andrea Mantegna
(Isola di Cartura, Padua, 1431-Mantua 1506)

Saint George

Panel, cm 66 × 32
(cat. 588)
Acquisition: 1856, by acquisition of the Manfrin collection
Latest restoration: 1992

Dated about 1446, this painting is believed to have been the side panel of a polyptych. The stern young man – more mythical hero than christian saint – wears a breast-plate inspired by a drawing of Jacopo Bellini, Mantegna's father-in-law.

4

Cosmè Tura
(Ferrara,1430-1495)

Madonna with Child

Panel, cm 61 × 41
(cat. 628)
Acquisition: 1896,
purchased
Latest restoration: 1982

A work of the founder of 15th-Century Ferrarese painting, dated between 1459 and 1463, this painting was probably conceived for a private residence, as the inscription near the bottom would indicate. The presence of profane elements in a sacred painting, including references to astrology, reflects an intellectual custom of the time and is recurrent in Ferrarese painting.

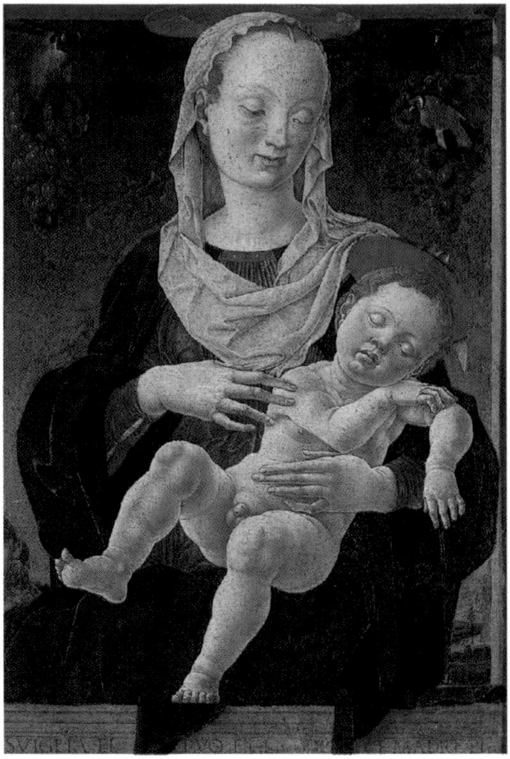

Giovanni Bellini
(Venice 1434/39-1516)

Pietà

Panel, cm 65 × 87
(cat. 883)
Acquisition: 1934, from the Donà delle Rose collection, following a convention
Latest restoration: 1996

A work commissioned for private use, Bellini's *Pietà* dates to the beginning of the 16th Century and is signed near the bottom on the left side. Rich with religious symbolism, the landscape brings together edifices of various origin in suggestive synthesis.

Giovanni Bellini
(Venice 1434/39-1516)

Madonna with Child with Saints Catherine and Magdalene

Panel, cm 107 × 58 (cat. 613)
Acquisition: 1850, by bequest of Felicita Renier
Latest restoration: 1997

Dated around 1500, this painting reflects the influence of Leonardo in its treatment of the relationship between background and subject. Dressed with refined elegance, the two saints seem more like two Venetian patricians than celestial creatures.

4

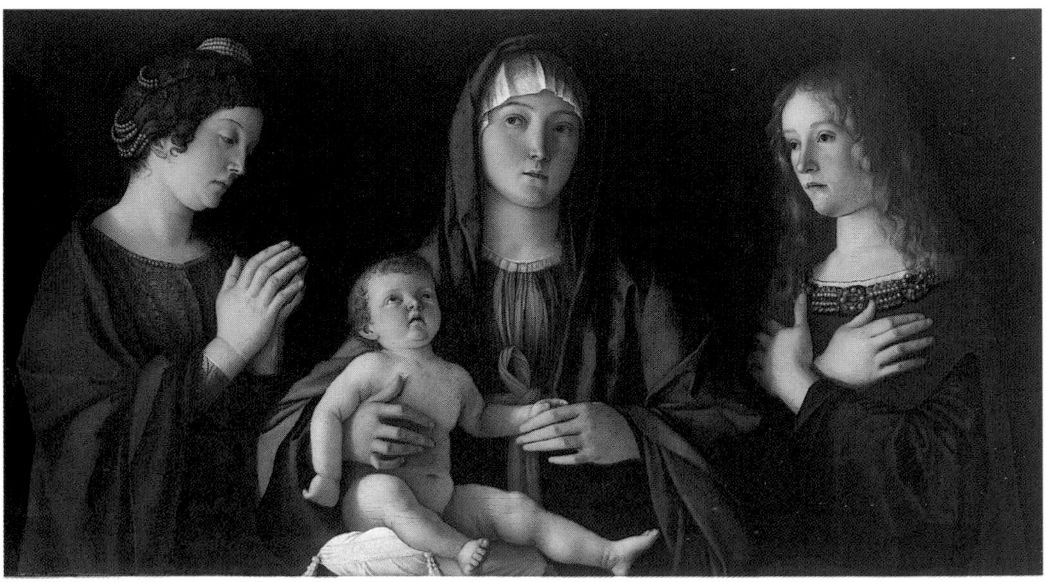

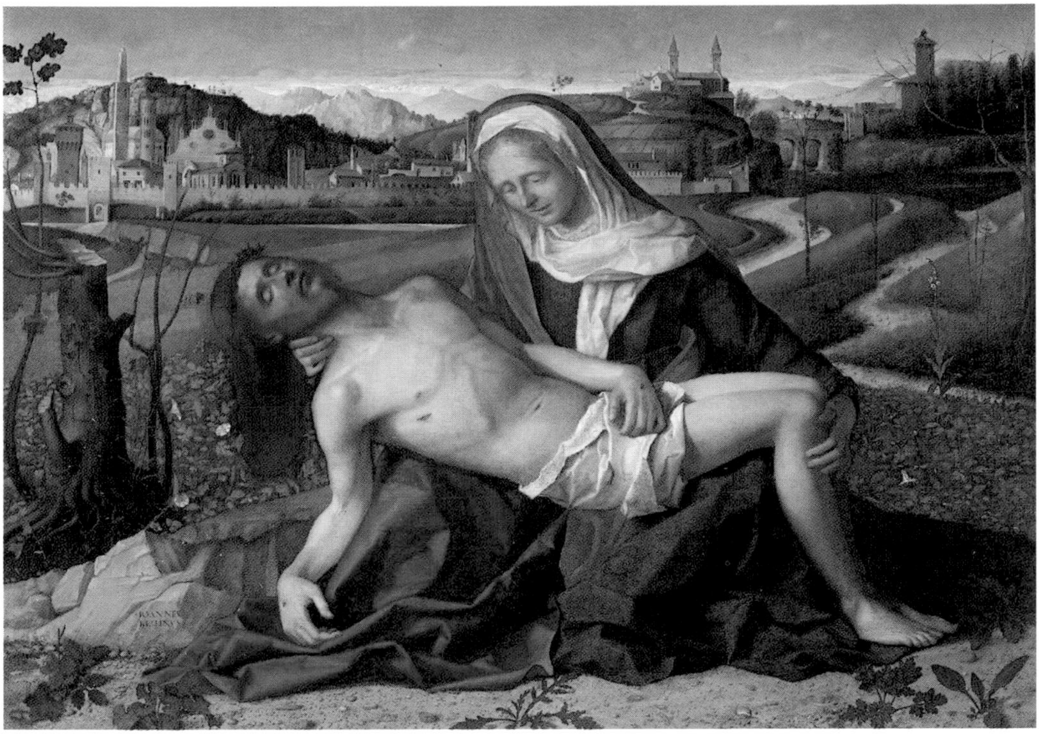

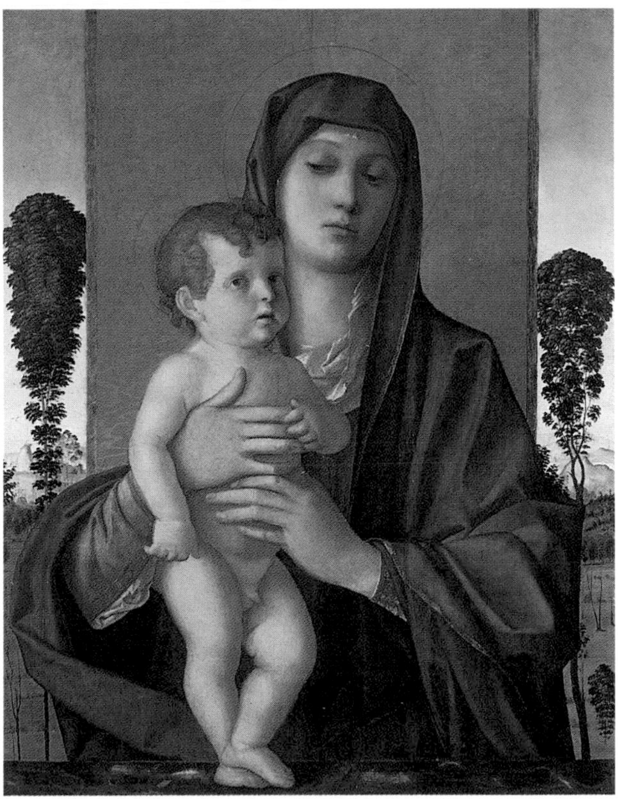

Giovanni Bellini
(Venice 1434/39-1516)

Madonna degli Alberetti
(Madonna of the Trees)

Panel, cm 71 × 58
(cat. 596)
Acquisition: 1938,
donated by Girolamo
Contarini.
Latest restoration: 1997

The first dated work by Giovanni Bellini (the date 1487 and Bellini's signature can be seen near the bottom in the centre), this is one of his most moving works for private devotion.

Giorgione
(Castelfranco 1476/77 -Venice 1510)

The Old Woman

Canvas, cm 68 × 59 (cat. 272)
Acquisition: 1856, by acquisition of the Manfrin collection.
Latest restoration: 1984

The interpretation of this work is extremely controversial: it is clearly an allegory, as the writing on the scroll, "col tempo" ("with time"), would indicate; but the symbolism notwithstanding, it is an extraordinary portrait in its own right.

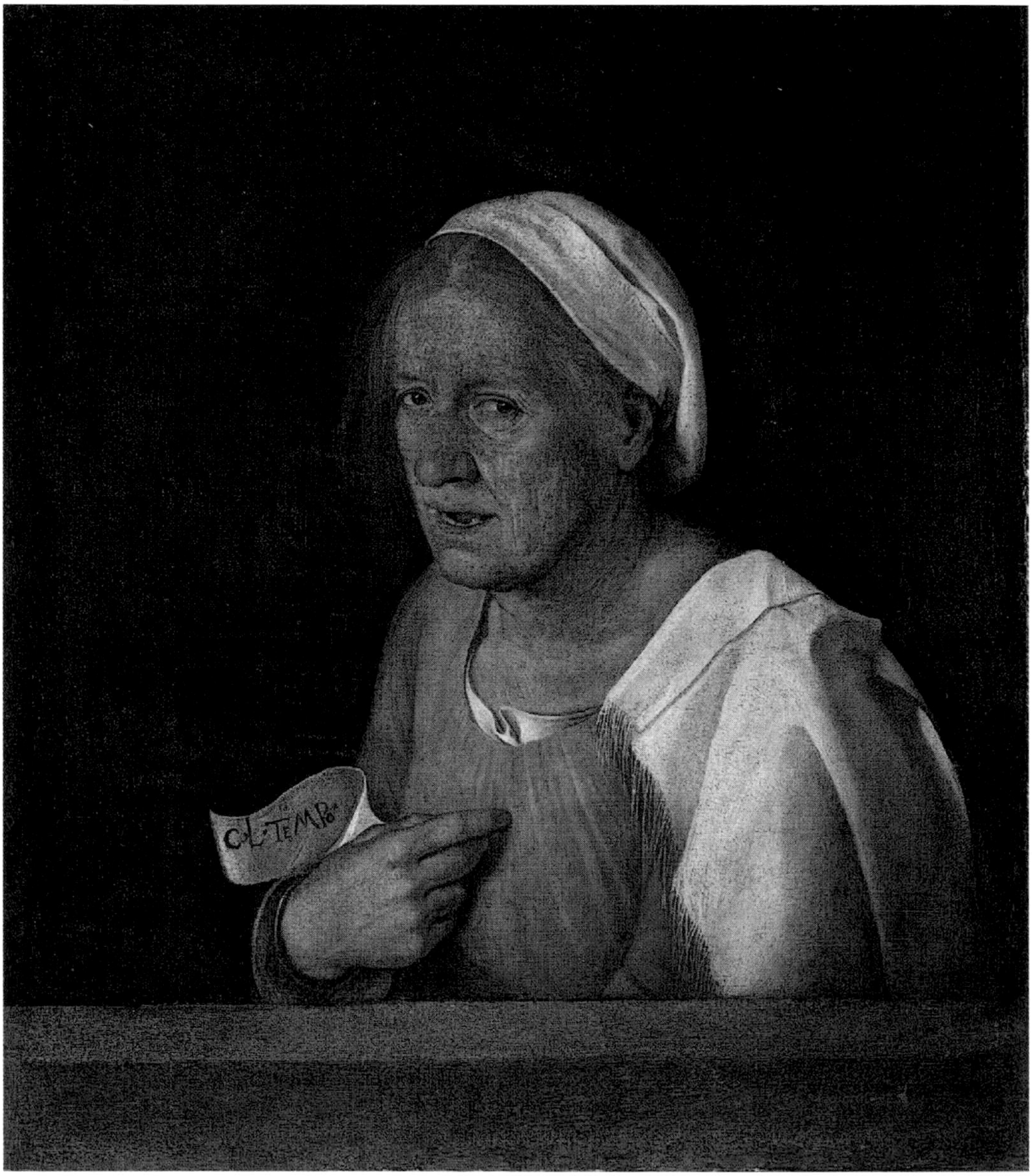

Giorgione
(Castelfranco 1476/77
-Venice 1510)

La Tempesta

Canvas, cm 82 × 73
(cat. 915)
Acquisition: 1932,
purchased from Prince
Alberto Giovanelli
Latest restoration: 1984

A private devotional work, the *Tempesta* has been the source of countless interpretations, from mythological to allegorical and even political. It has also been seen as the melding of many literary and figurative sources, or even as a work which would not require any decoding whatsoever, representing simply what Michiel has suggested: a "tempest" with a gypsy.

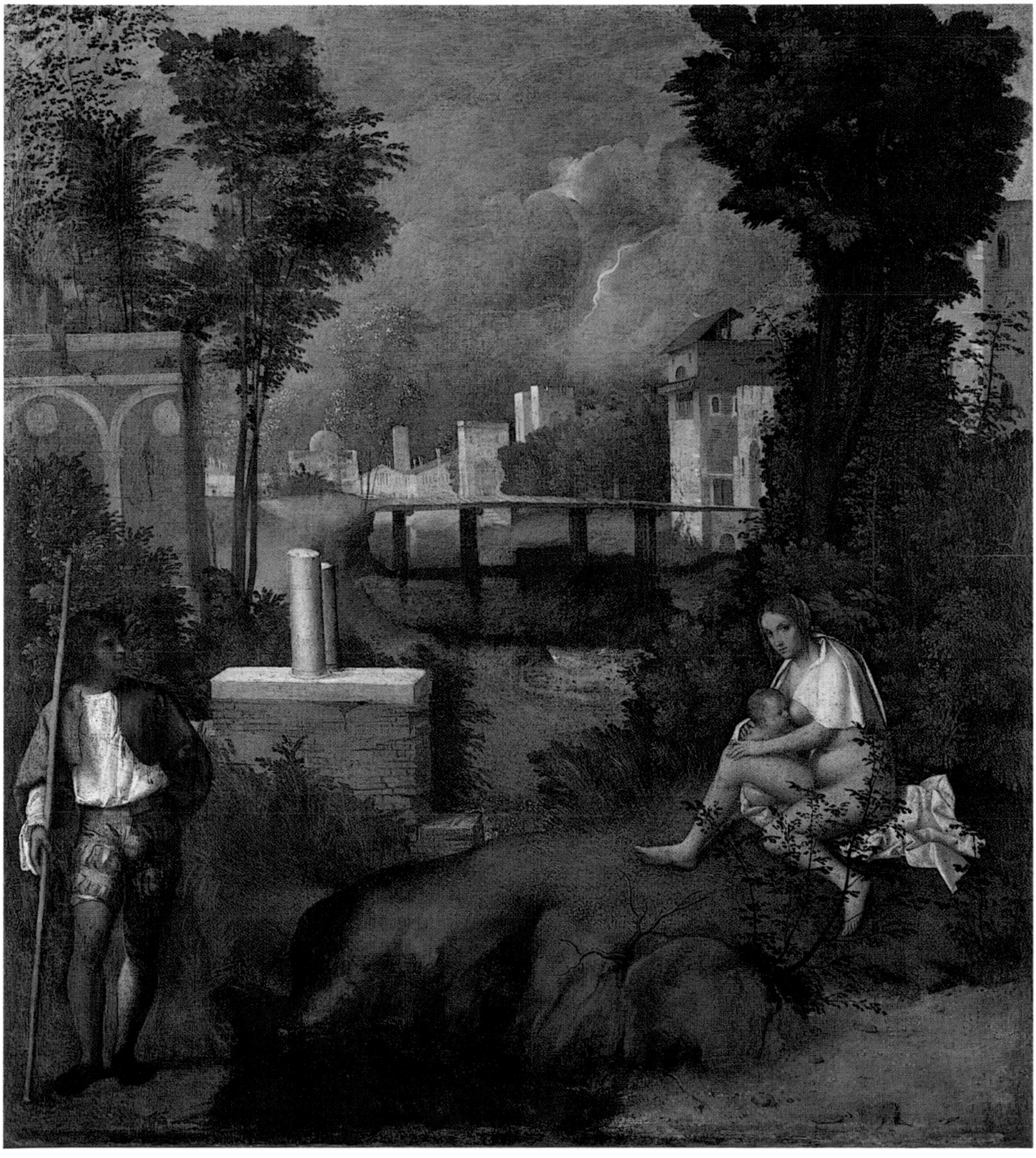

5

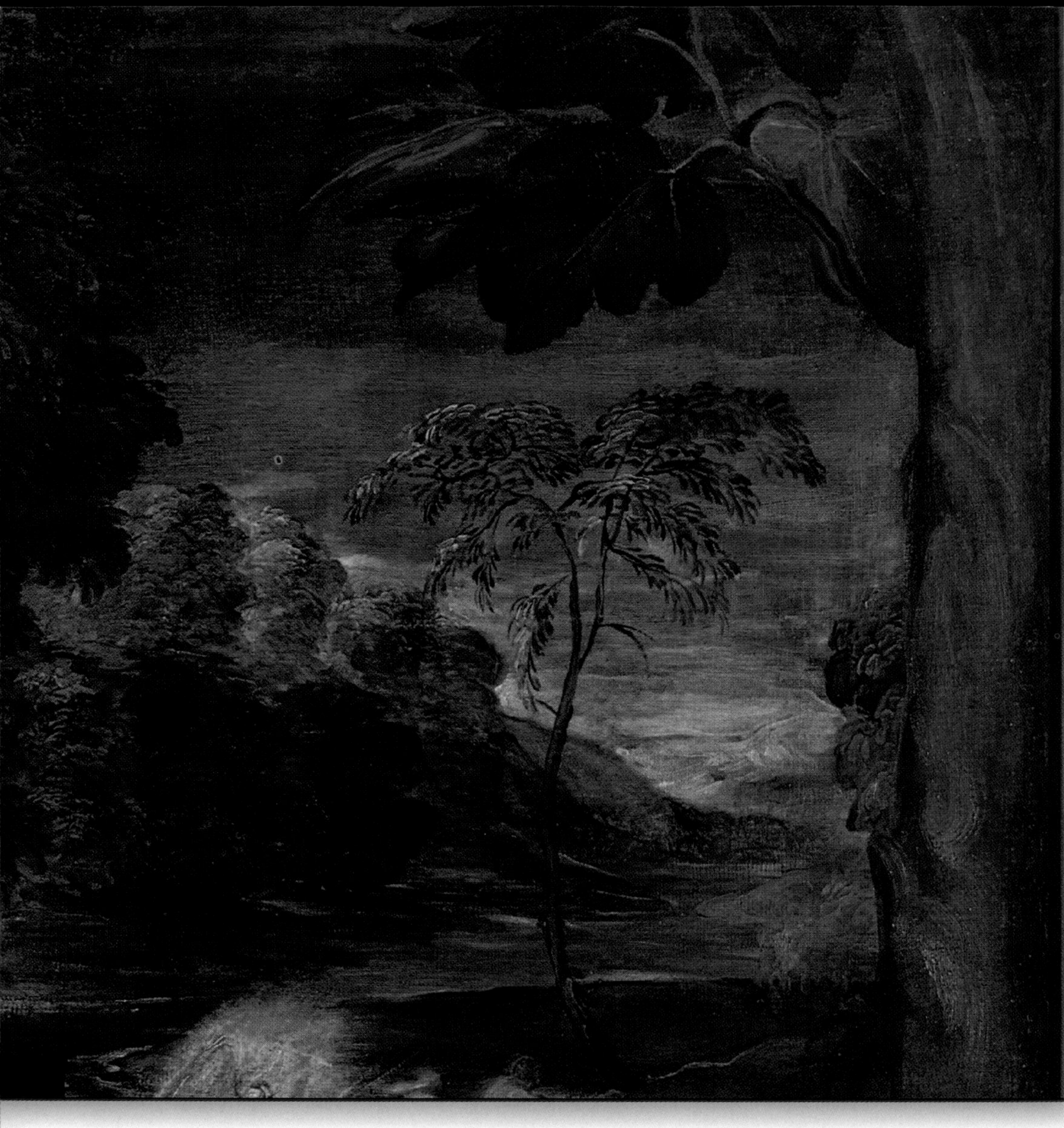

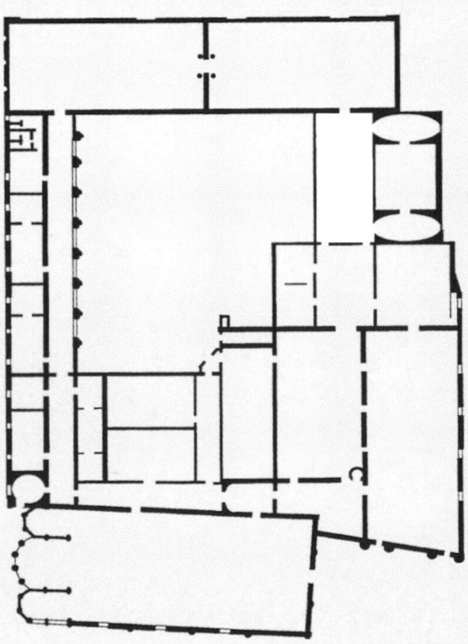

Room **6**

Titian, Jacopo Tintoretto and Paolo Veronese

In this room are displayed works by Tiziano Vecellio (Titian), Jacopo Robusti (Tintoretto) and Paolo Caliari (Veronese).
In 2000 two walled windows were reopened, enabling to see the façade of the Palladian convent.

Titian
(Pieve di Cadore c. 1488/90-Venice 1576)
Saint John the Baptist
Canvas, cm 201 × 119 (cat. 314)
Acquisition: 1808
Latest restoration: 1981

Signed "Ticianus" on the stone at the bottom, this painting was originally located in the church of Santa Maria Maggiore. The figure of the saint – from the stunning preparatory sketch – recalls both Michelangelo and classical art sources, while the background landscape is decidedly fresh and new.

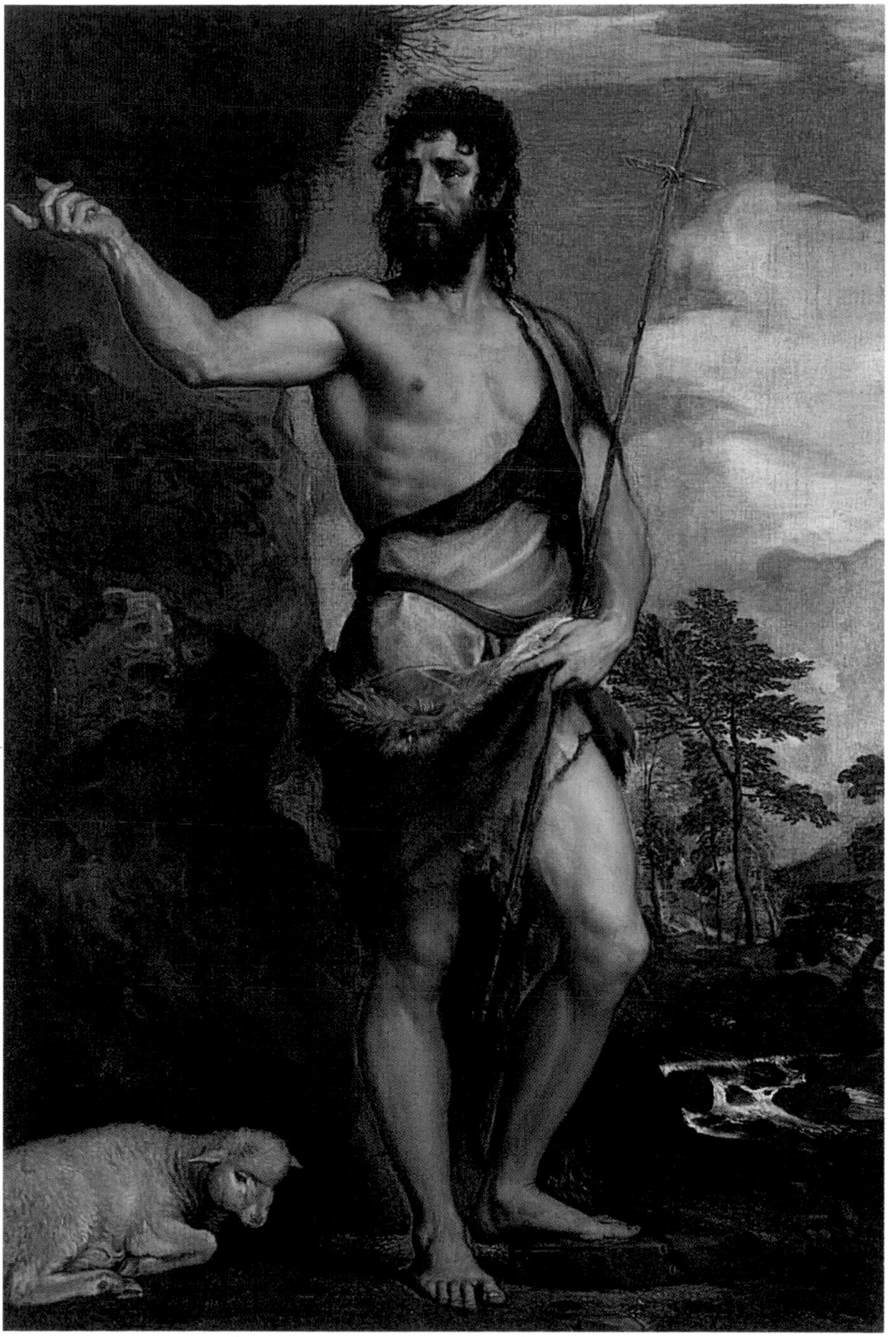

6

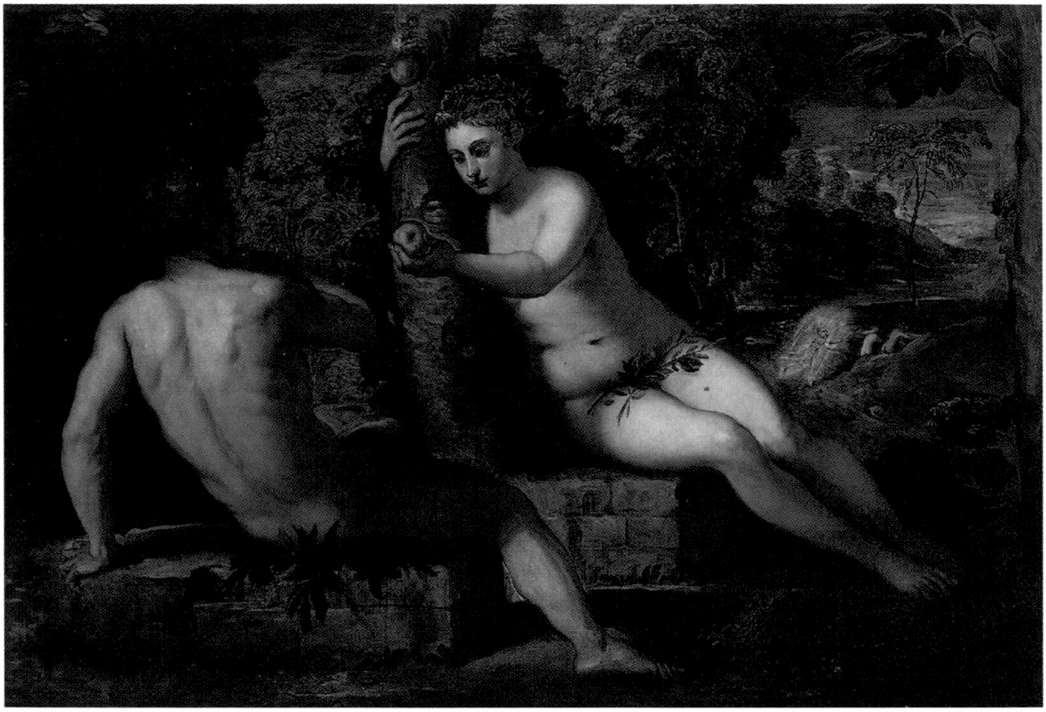

6

Jacopo Robusti (Tintoretto)
(Venice 1519-1594)

The Temptation of Adam and Eve

Canvas, cm 150 × 220
(cat. 43)
Acquisition: 1812, following the Napoleonic suppressions
Latest restoration: 1967

This work, together with the *Creation of the Animals* and *Cain and Abel*, created sometime between 1550 and 1553, was originally in the Scuola della Trinità. Adam and Eve are captured just before the consummation of their sin; to the right the sin has already been committed and the two progenitors are chased out by the angel.

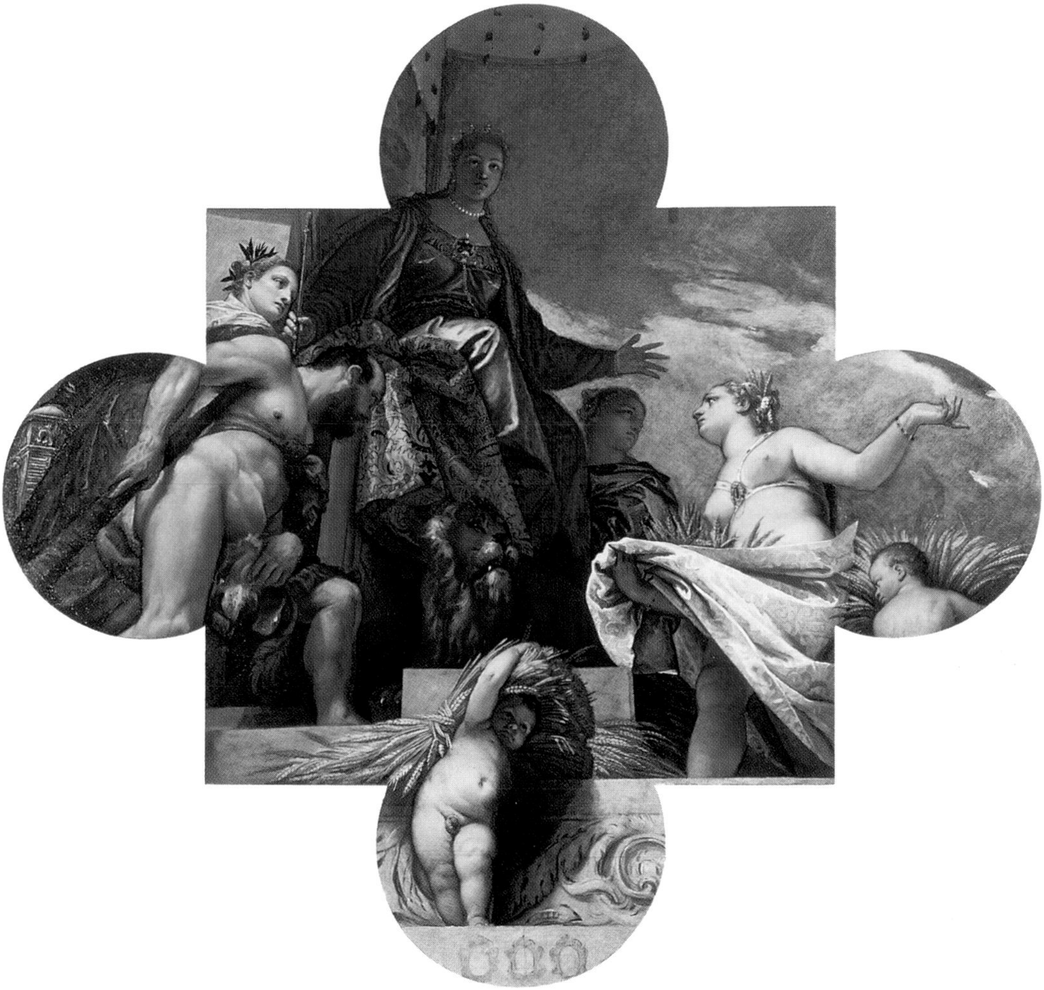

6

Paolo Caliari (Veronese)
(Verona 1528-Venice 1588)

Venice receives tribute from Hercules and Ceres

Canvas, cm 308 × 327
(ct. 45)
Acquisition: 1895
Latest restoration: 1986

When once kept in the Doges Palace, in the "Magistrato alle Biade", the painting was perhaps rectangular. Dated at around 1576-78, it is one of the artists fundamental works due to the skillful perspective, backlighting effects and refined colouring.

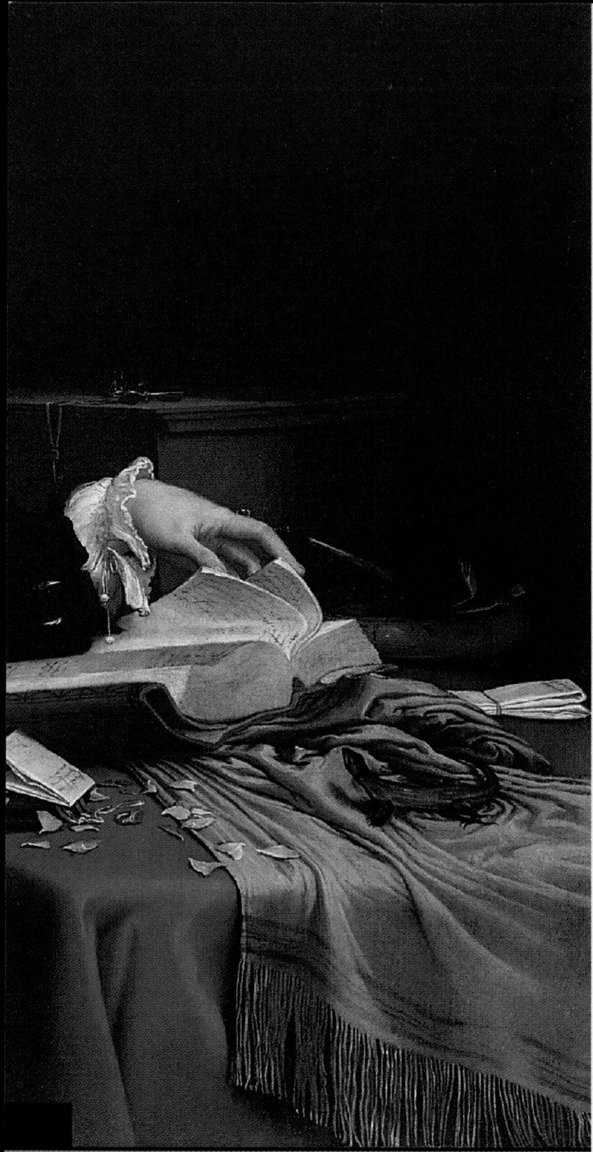

Lorenzo Lotto, Romanino and Jacopo Palma il Vecchio

In these rooms are displayed works by Giovanni Busi (Cariani), Antonio Badile, Giovanni Girolamo Savoldo, Alessandro Bonvicino (il Moretto), Bernardino Licinio, Lorenzo Lotto, Jacopo Negretti (Palma il Vecchio), Tiziano Vecellio (Titian), Bonifacio de'Pitati (Bonifacio Veronese), Giorgio Vasari, Andrea Previtali, Girolamo Romani (il Romanino) and the 16th-Century Venetian school.

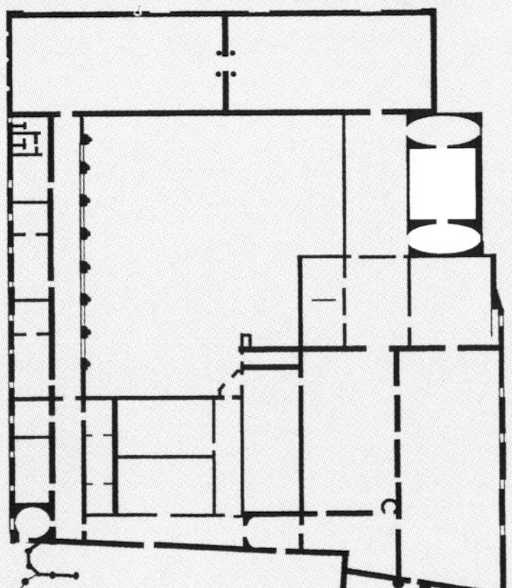

Lorenzo Lotto
(Venice c. 1480-Loreto 1556)

Portrait of a Gentleman in his Study

Canvas, cm 97 × 110
(cat. 912)
Acquisition: 1930, purchased
Latest restoration: 1997

Dating about 1528, this is one of the most famous portraits by Lotto. The young man is captured as a thought distracts him from his reading; his pallid face emerging from the darkness reveals a psychological intensity that foreshadows modern portraiture.

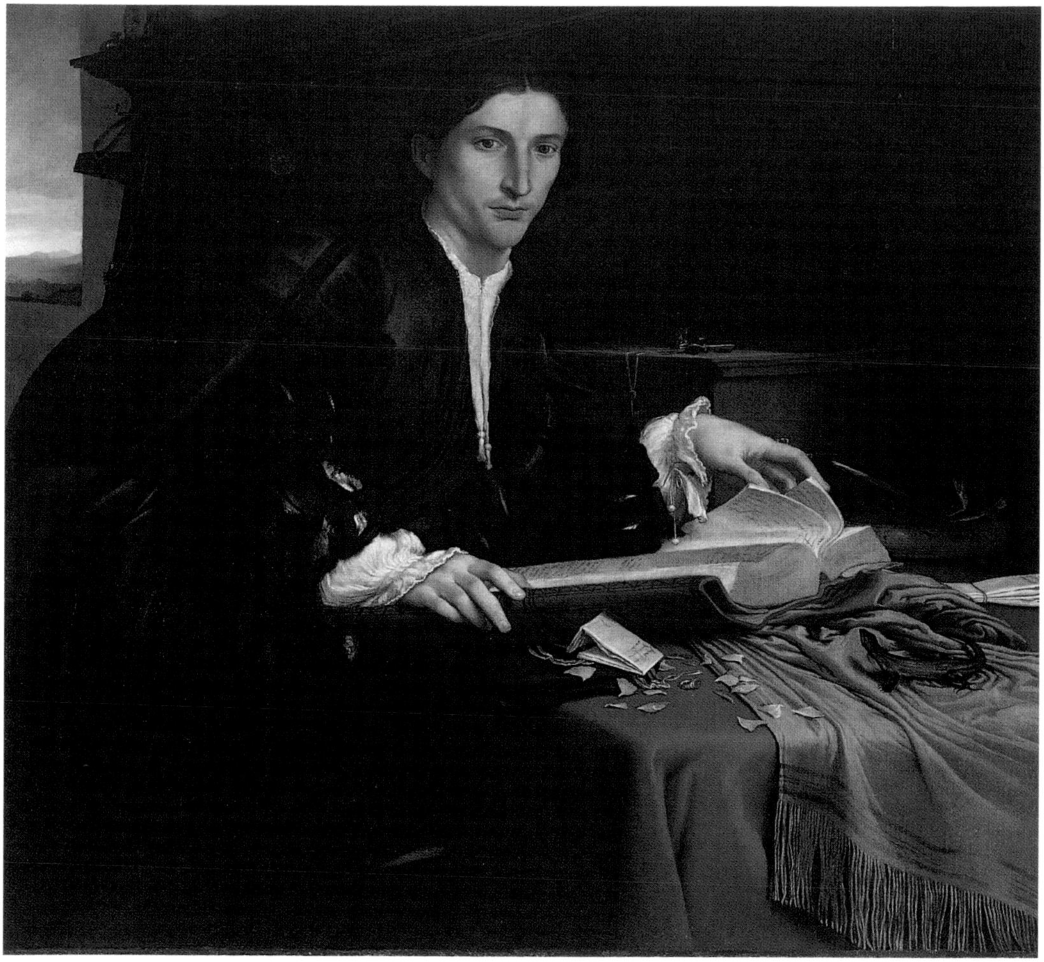

7

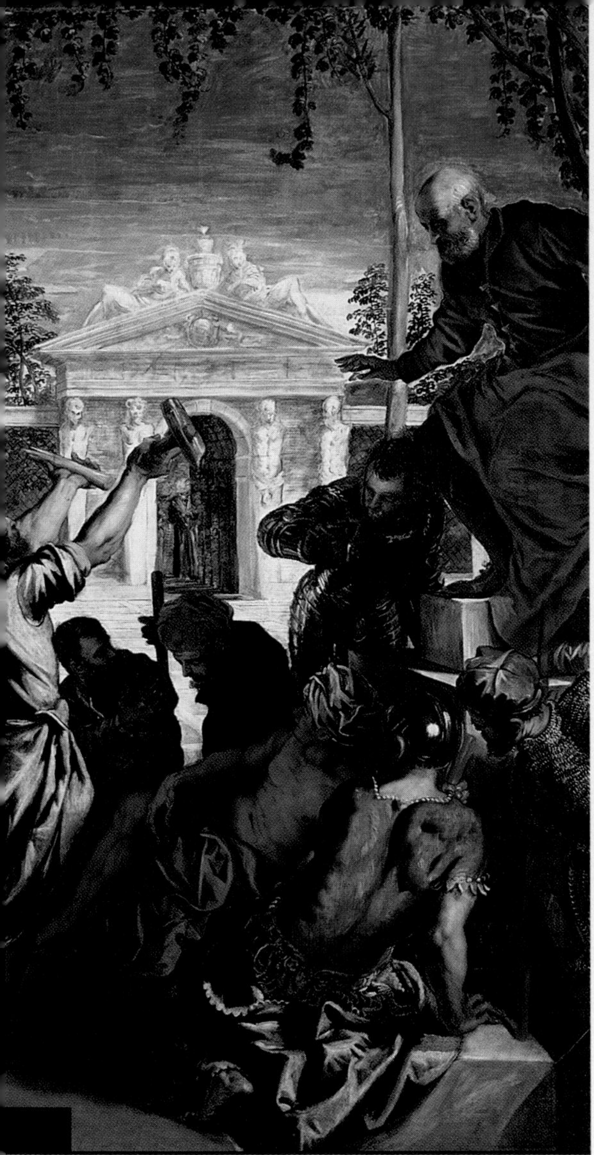

Titian, Jacopo Tintoretto and Paolo Veronese

Begun by Francesco Lazzari in 1828, the room was inaugurated in 1834. The passage between this room and its twin hall (room 11) is decorated with four columns in Greek marble from the Scuola di Santa Maria della Misericordia.
In this room are shown works by Paolo Caliari (Veronese), Jacopo Robusti (Tintoretto) and Tiziano Vecellio (Titian).

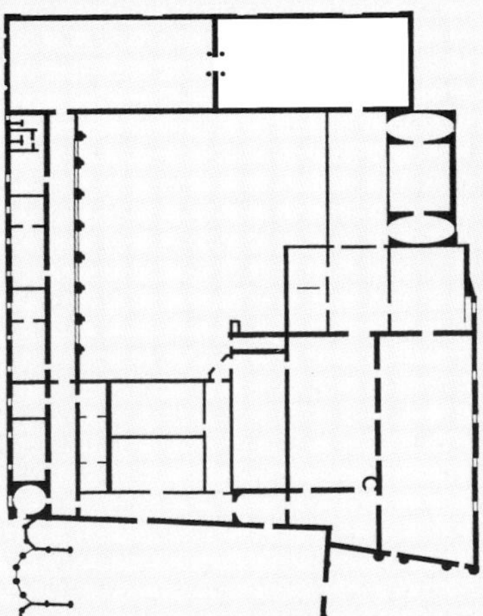

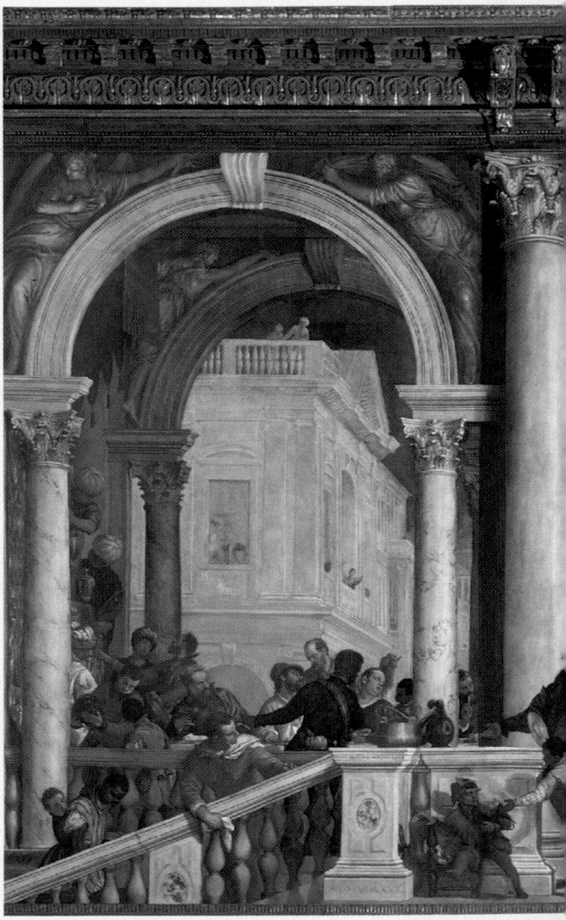

Paolo Caliari (Veronese)
(Verona 1528-Venice 1588)

Christ in the House of Levi

Canvas, cm 560 × 1309
(cat. 203)
Acquisition: 1815
Latest restoration: 1980-82

This great painting was originally a *Last Supper* for the refectory of the convent of Santi Giovanni e Paolo, as a replacement for a *Last Supper* by Titian which had been lost in a fire. The artist was accused of heresy for this vast composition which contained what were considered to be excessively anti-conformist elements.

Veronese was ordered to "amend" the painting, in line with canonical tradition. But the only change he made was to append the writing on the top of the pillar with the date below, changing the subject to the *Feast in the House of Levi* (Luke, V), who, being a Publican, could receive at his table a mixed crowd.

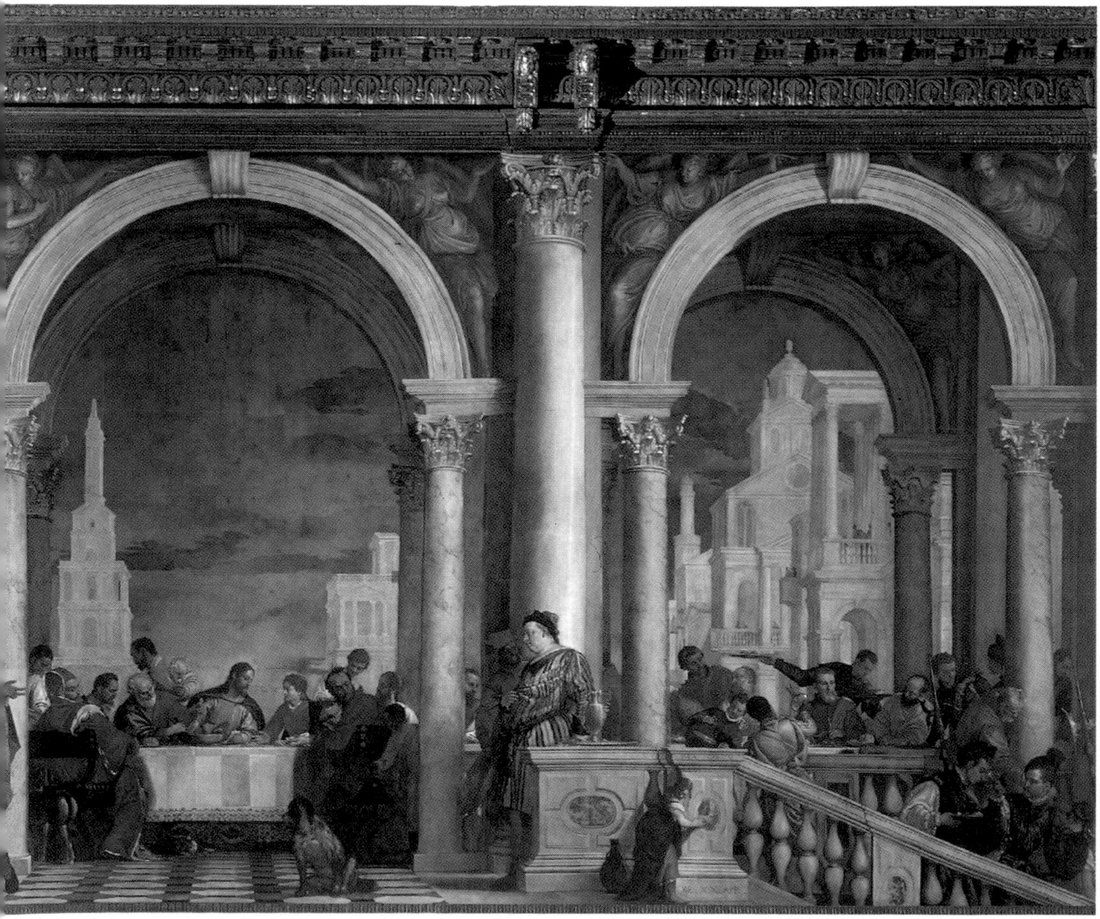

10

Jacopo Robusti (Tintoretto)
(Venice 1519-1594)

Miracle of Saint Mark Freeing the Slave

Canvas, cm 416 × 544
(cat. 42)
Acquisition: 1821
Latest restoration: 1965

This was the first painting made by Tintoretto for the Assembly Hall of the Scuola Grande di San Marco. It was probably commissioned in 1547 and completed by April of 1548 when Aretino, writing to Tintoretto, praised it. The scene is that of a slave being freed as a result of the intercession of Saint Mark: he had been sentenced to be blinded and his limbs broken because, against his master's wiel, he had gone to worship the saint's relies.

10

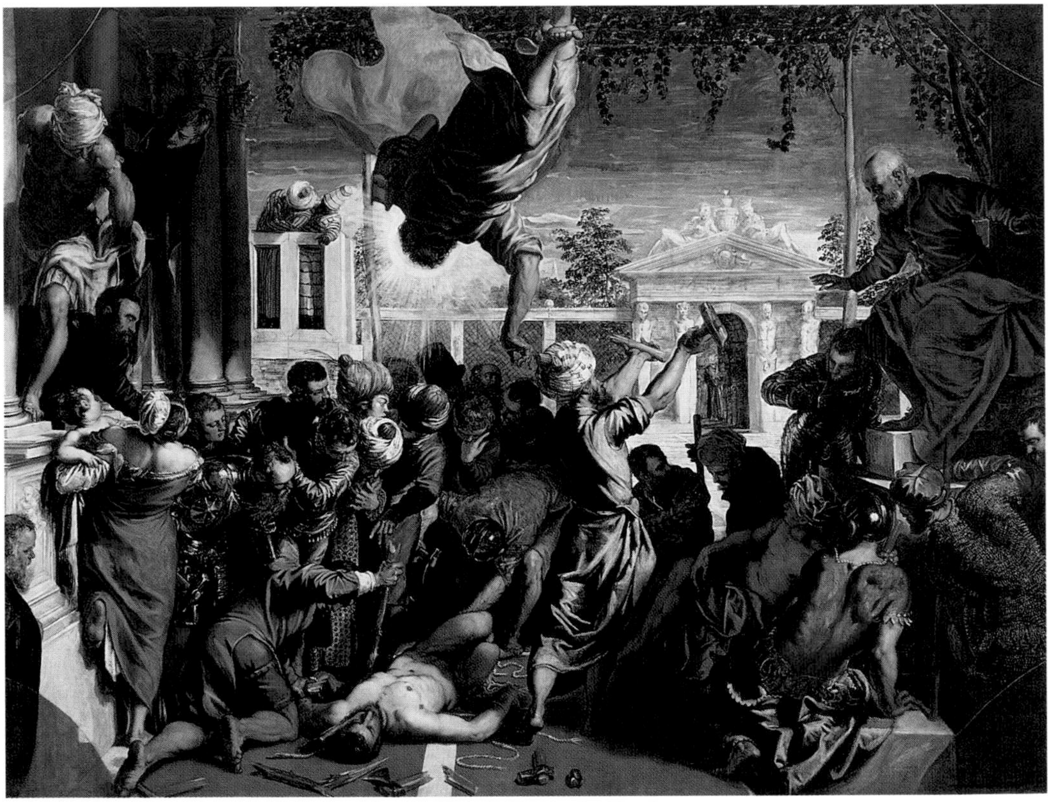

Jacopo Robusti (Tintoretto)
(Venice 1519-1594)

Transport of the Body of Saint Mark

Canvas, cm 397 × 315
(cat. 631)
Acquisition: 1920
Latest restoration: 1991-92

Painted between 1562 and 1566 for the Scuola Grande di San Marco, this work documents Tintoretto's imaginative and evocative style, and reveals the new "luminismo" which typifies Tintoretto's paintings from this period.

It represent, according to the legend, the episod during which two venitian tradesmen owing to a sudden storm, were able to remove Saint Mark's body that was about to be burned at the stake.

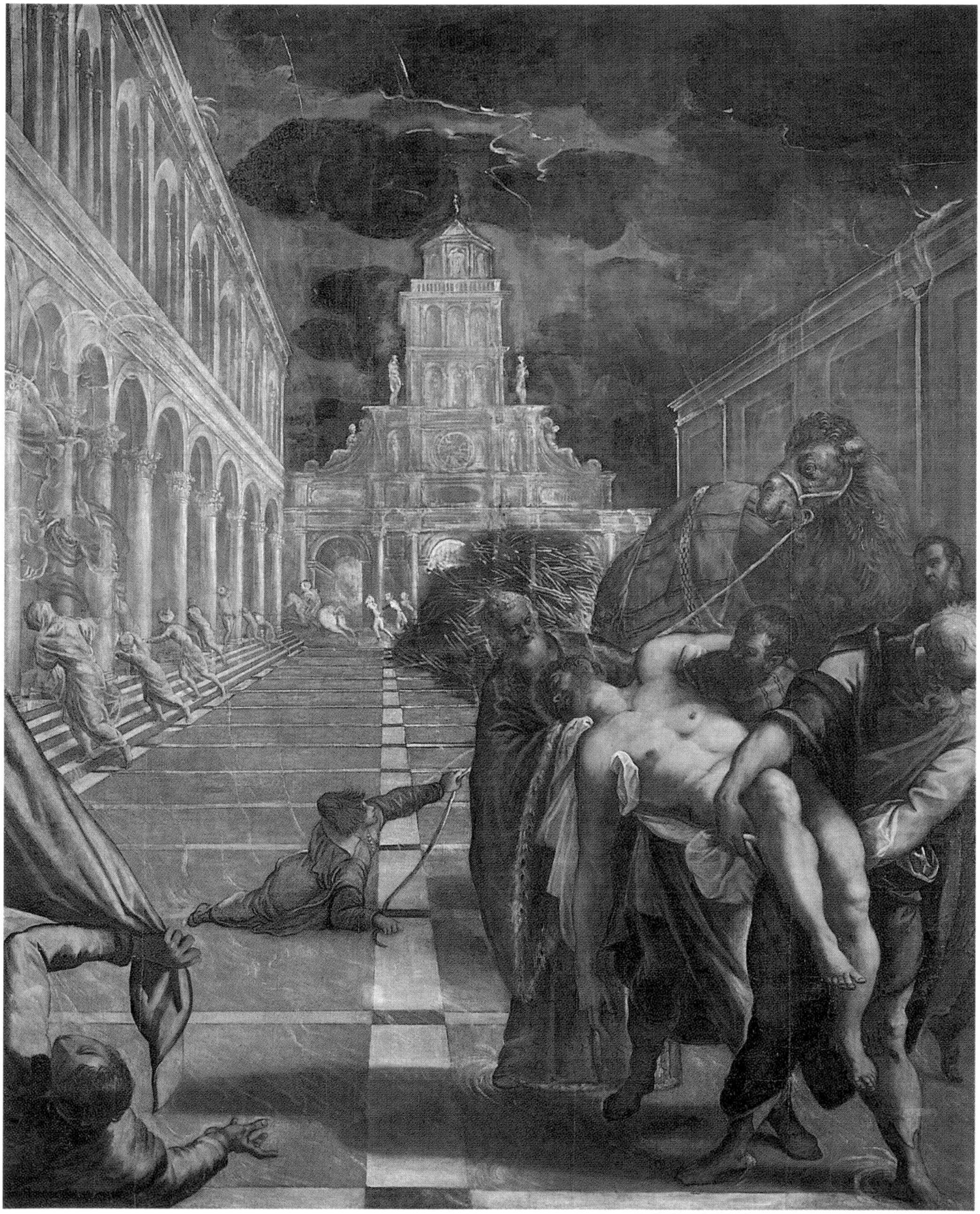

10

Paolo Caliari (Veronese)
(Verona 1528-Venice 1588)

The Marriage of Saint Catherine

Canvas, cm 377 × 241
(cat. 1324)
Acquisition: 1918

Latest restoration: 1986
Painted for the main altar of the Venetian church of Santa Caterina.
Dated around 1575, near the time when Veronese painted the canvases for the ceiling of the Collegio Hall in the Doge's Palace.

It represents Catherine of Alexandria's allegorical nuptials with Jesus, the only person worthy of being the spouse of a king's daughter, of great beauty and precocious wisdom.

10

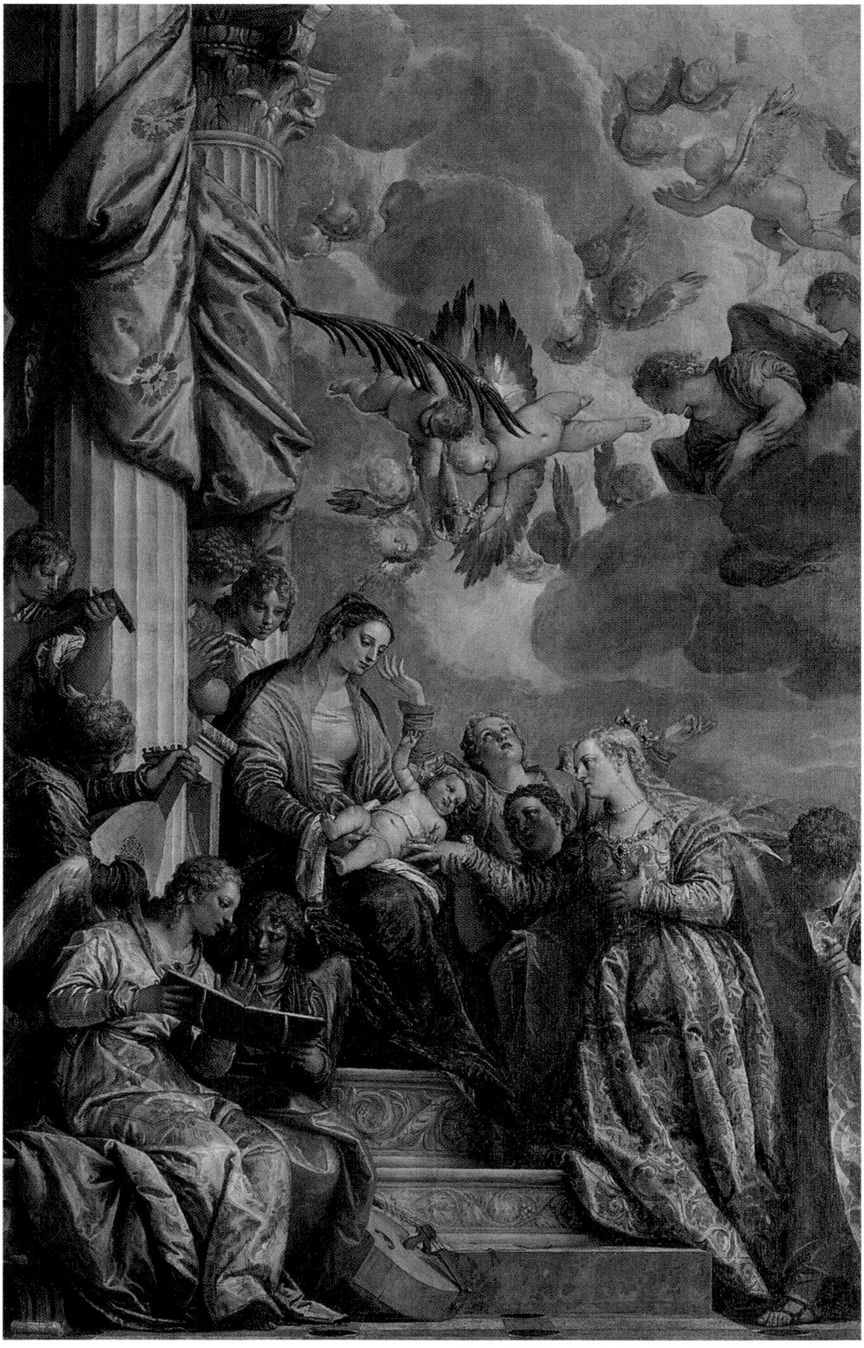

Titian
(Pieve di Cadore c. 1488/90-Venice 1576)

Pietà

Canvas, cm 353 × 347
(cat. 400)
Acquisition: 1814
Latest restoration: 1984-85

This work reached the Accademia from the church of Sant'Angelo, where it had been placed in 1631 at the end of the great plague. Conceived by Titien for the church of Frari in exchange for the concession for burial therein, it was briefly shown there in March 1575. In the course of 1575, during the spreading of the pestilence, the artist was to nearly transform it into a huge ex-voto, producing an exceptional autobiographic document. As the writing near the bottom attests, the work was definitively completed by Jacopo Palma il Giovane. The old man lying prostrate in front of the Virgin – probably Nicodemus – is a self-portrait of Titian.

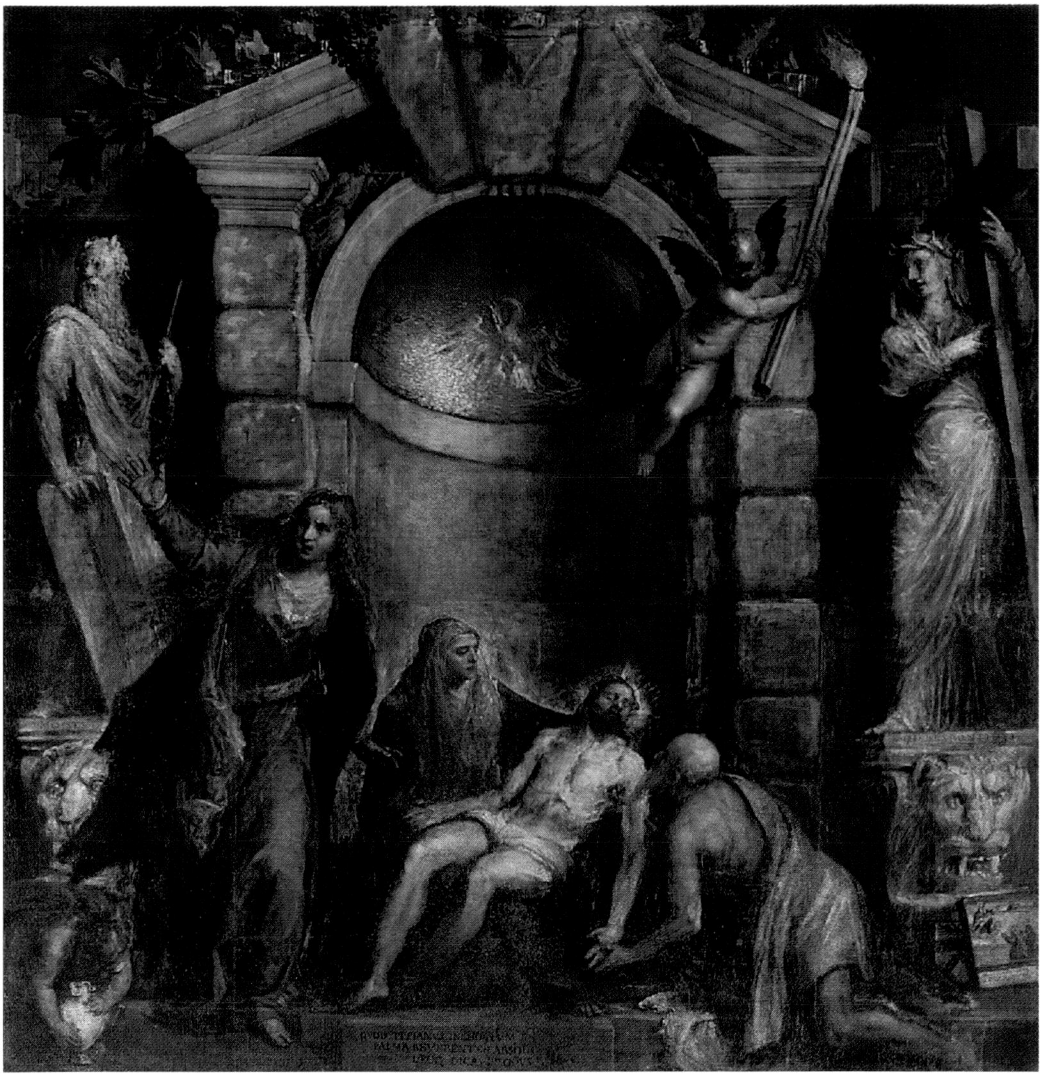

10

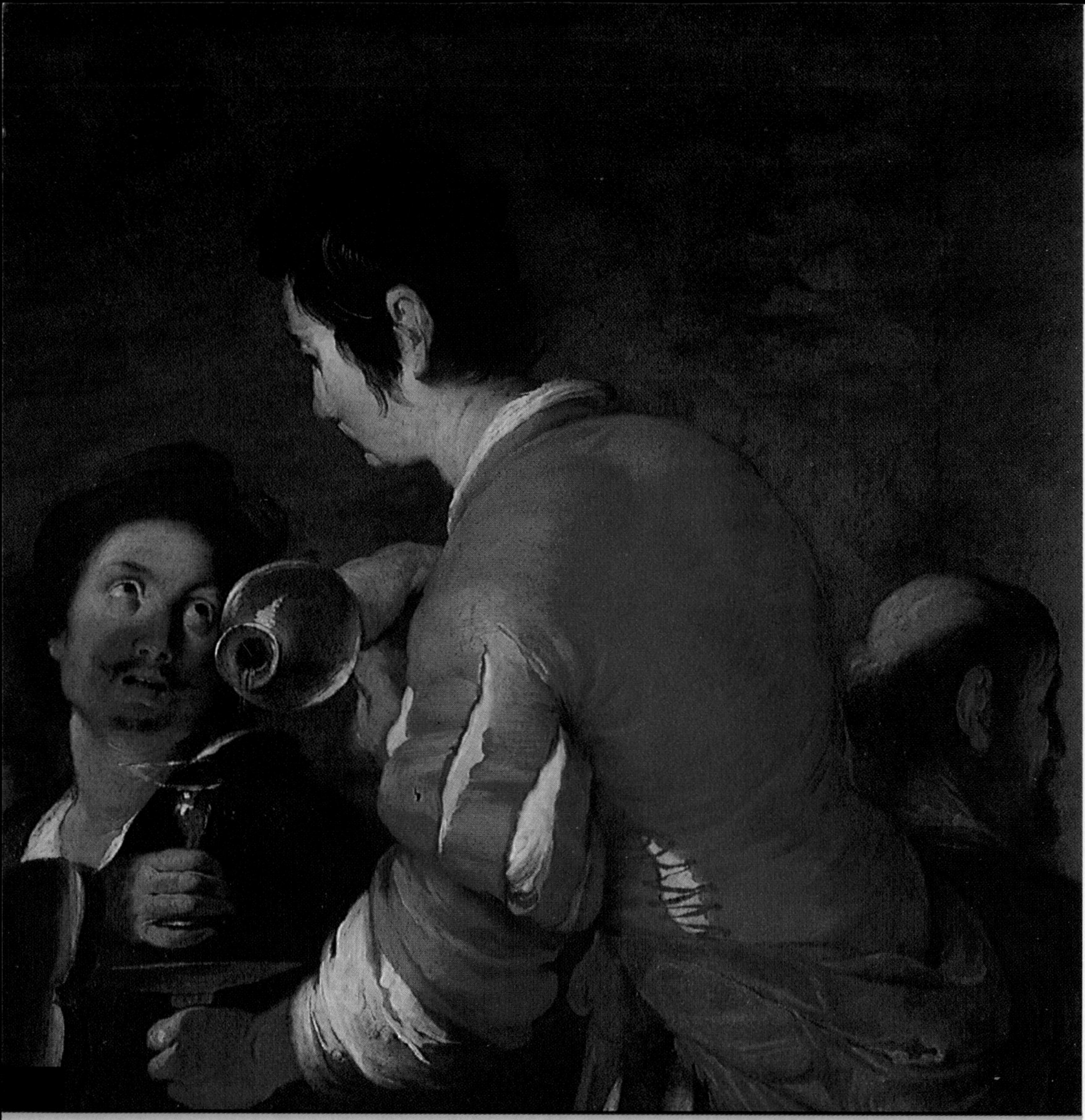

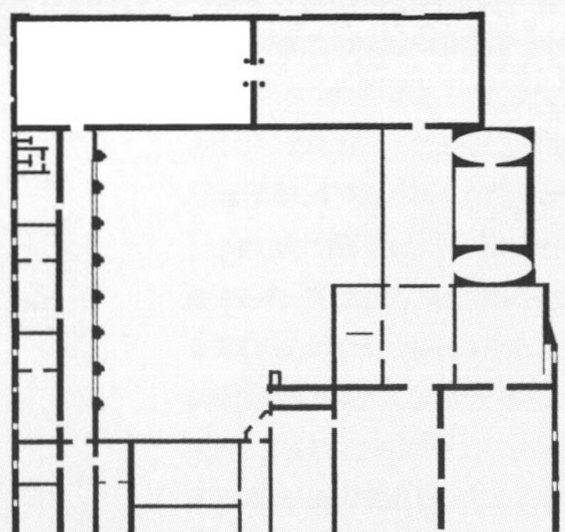

Bonifacio Veronese, Jacopo Tintoretto, Bernardo Strozzi and Giambattista Tiepolo

In this room are shown works by Leandro da Ponte (Bassano), Bernardo Strozzi, Giambattista Tiepolo, Luca Giordano, Jacopo Robusti (Tintoretto), Bonifacio de' Pitati (Bonifacio Veronese), Giovanni Antonio de' Sacchis (Pordenone).

Bernardo Strozzi
(Genoa 1581-Venice 1644)

Portrait of the Knight Giovanni Grimani

Canvas, cm 225 × 143
(cat. 1358)
Acquisition: 1981
Latest restoration: 1995

Giovanni Grimani, while he was ambassador in Vienna from 1636 to 1640, was knighted by the Emperor. He is portrayed with the golden stole, symbol of the knighthood. This work is a masterpiece from the height of Strozzi's artistic maturity. Hints of Rubens and Van Dyck are brought together with a decidedly Venetian treatment of light and colour.

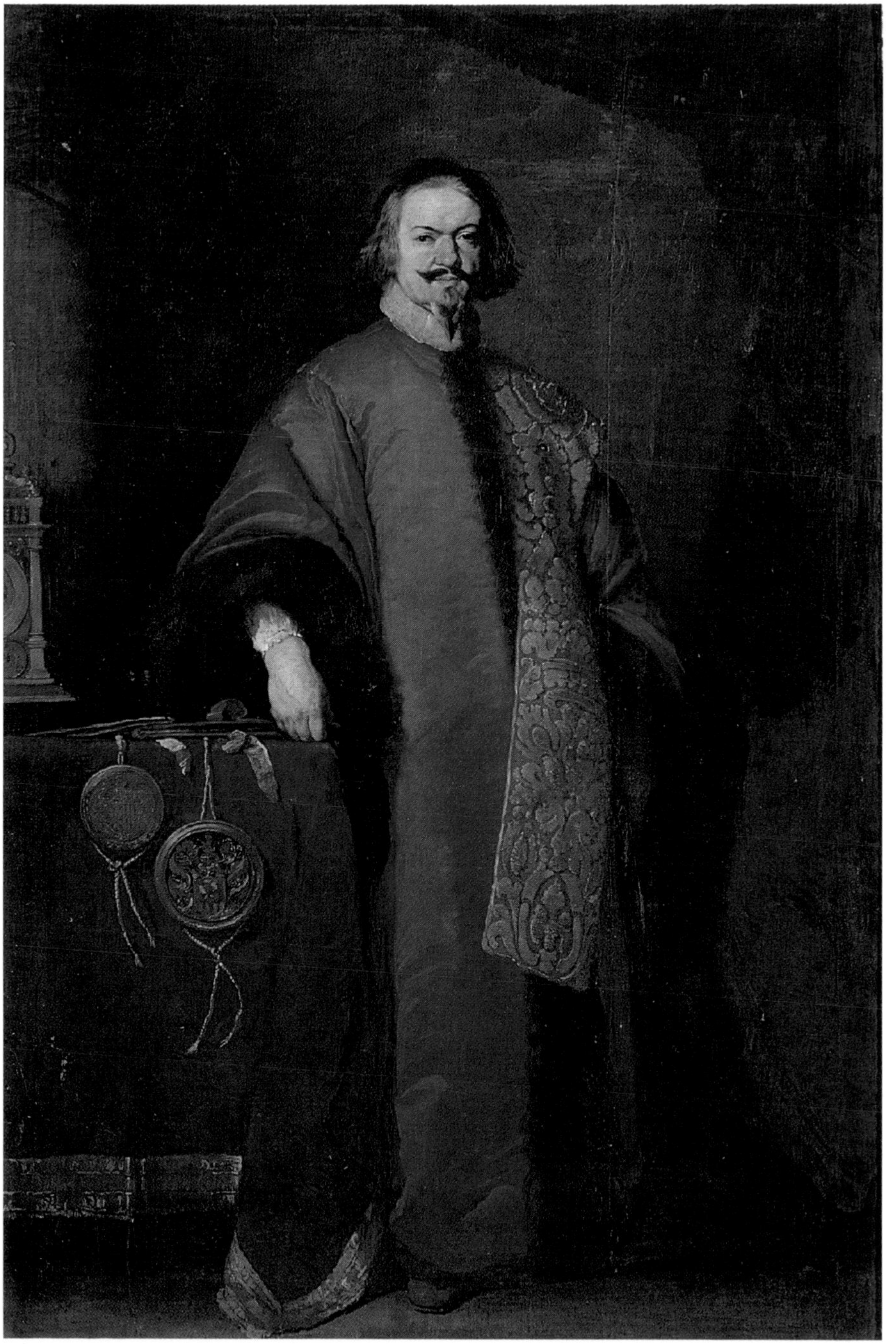

11

Giambattista Tiepolo
(Venice 1696-Madrid 1770)

Discovery the True Cross

Canvas, 500 cm diameter (cat. 462)
Acquisition: 1812
Latest restoration: 1982

The large ceiling painting was made for the church of Le Cappuccine in Castello, which was destroyed. A sketch showing an early idea for the painting is also in the Accademia (cat. 789, room 17).

Bernardo Strozzi
(Genoa 1581- Venice 1644)

Feast in the House of Simon

Canvas, cm 257 × 737 (cat. 777)
Acquisition: 1911
Latest restoration: 1981

This large painting from the chapel of Palazzo Gorleri in Genoa reveals a distinct Venetian influence, a style well known to Strozzi even before he moved to Venice.

11

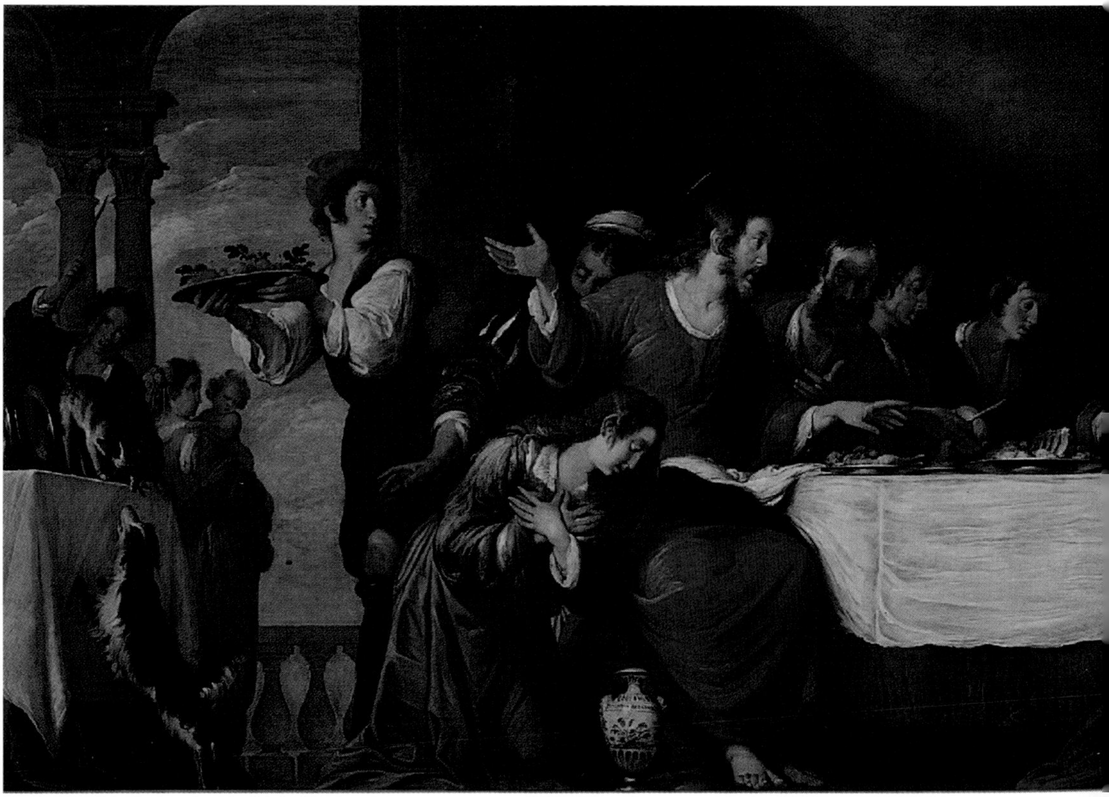

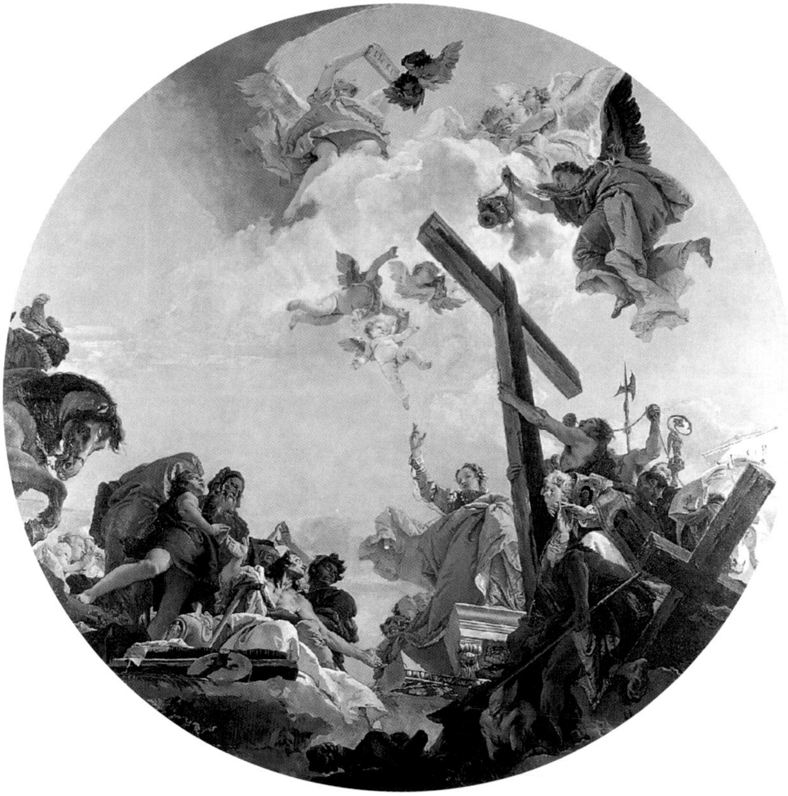

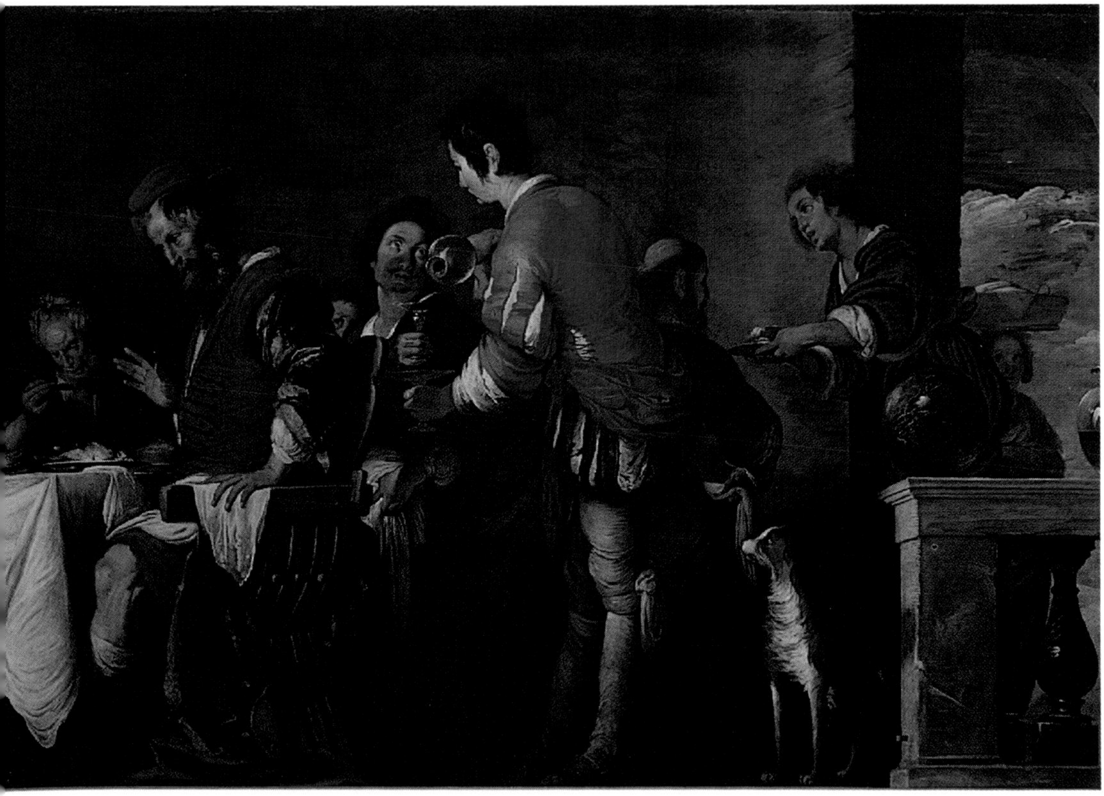

11

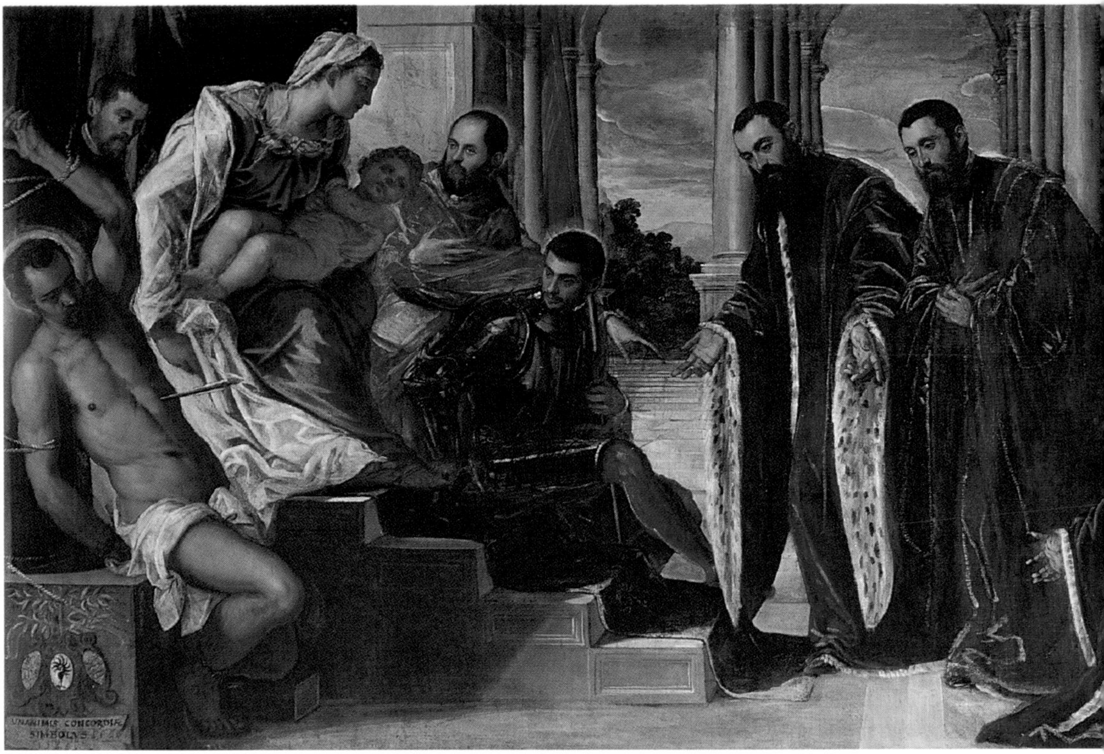

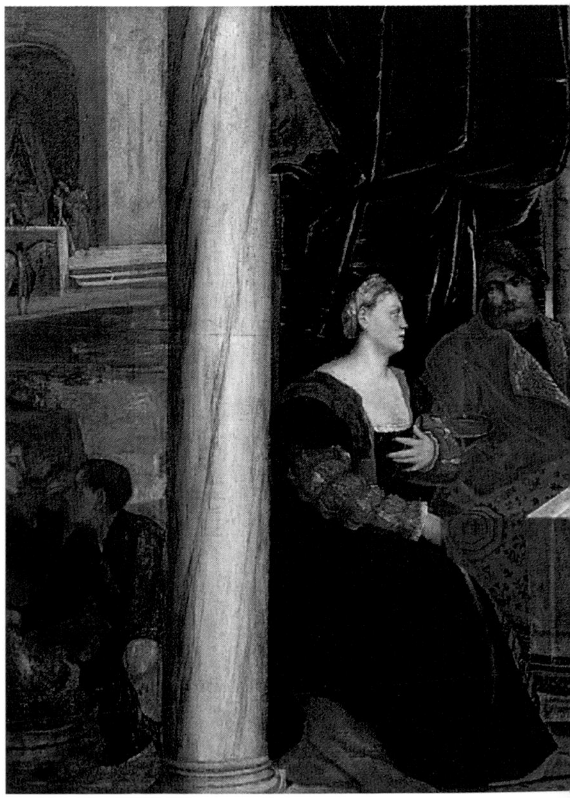

11

Bonifacio de' Pitati (Bonifacio Veronese)
(Verona 1487-Venice 1553)

The wealthy Epulon

Canvas, cm 206 × 438
(cat. 291)
Acquisition: 1812
Latest restoration: 1991-92

Dated around 1543-1545, this is the artist's masterpiece. The episode of Epulon refusing to give alms to poor Lazarus becomes the pretext for an extraordinary description of Venetian villa life.

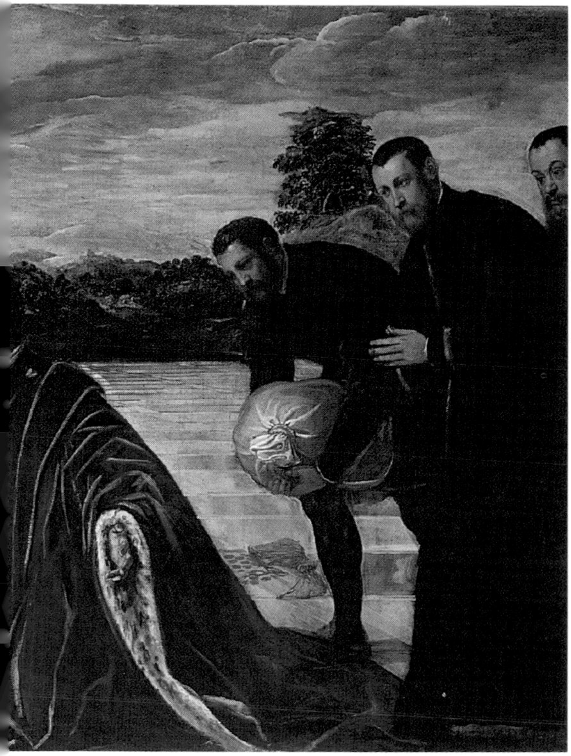

Jacopo Robusti (Tintoretto)
(Venice 1519-1594)
Madonna dei Camerlenghi
Canvas, cm 221 × 520
(cat. 210)
Acquisition: 1883
Latest restoration: 1992

This large painting was made in 1567 for the Camerlenghi palazzo at the Rialto. It is a masterpiece of the Venetian votive painting tradition.

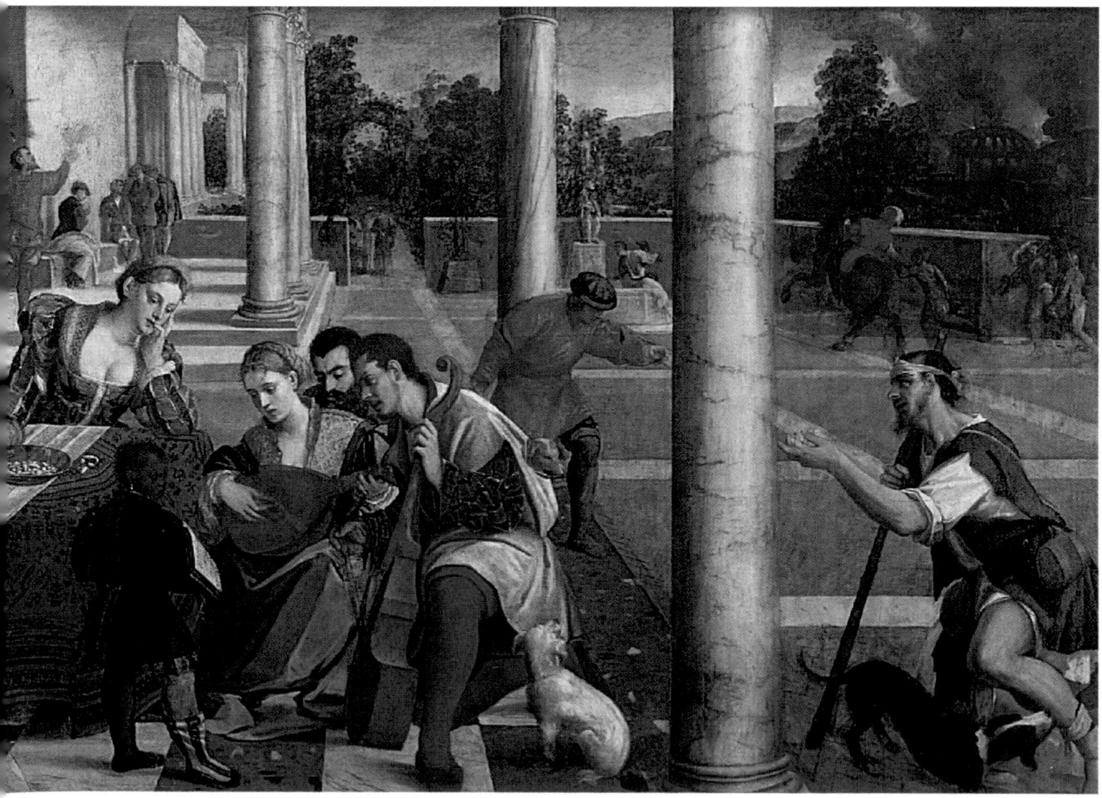

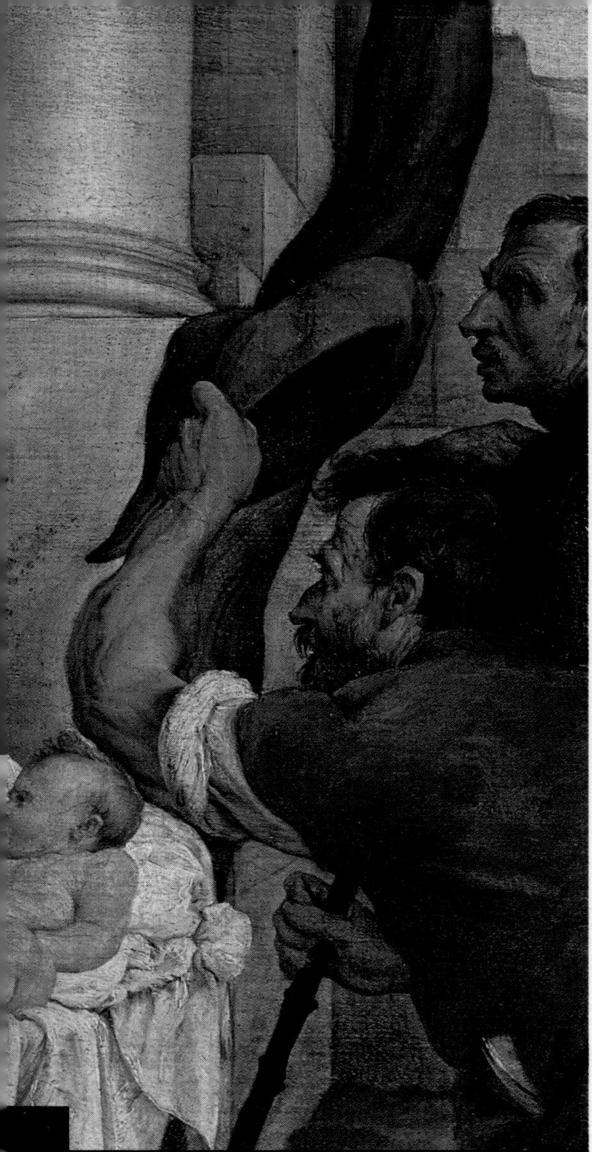

Marco Ricci, Francesco Zuccarelli, Giuseppe Zais, Jacopo Bassano and portraits by Jacopo Tintoretto

Room 12. The hall is made up of the long Palladian corridor, with its grand windows (probably dating back to Lazzari during the 1800's). In 1912, three doors were added with their oversections – perhaps taken from a palazzo in Brescia, as they are the work of Pietro Scalvini (Brescia 1718-92) and Saverio Gandini (Cremona ca. 1729–Brescia 1796). In the door where the sculpture is depicted we can see the signature of Scalvini and the date 1778. The hall also displays works by Marco Ricci, Giuseppe Zais, Francesco Zuccarelli and Antonio Diziani.

Room 13. Obtained by joining three rooms of the Carità convent, with the earliest restoration works, the ceiling of the first zone, which was decorated by Tranquillo Orsi, was uncovered after some years under a large canvas. Later in 1947, Carlo Scarpa undertook more work on it. On display in the hall are works by Jacopo da Ponte (Bassano), Jacopo Robusti (Tintoretto), Andrea Michieli (il Vicentino), Jacopo Negretti (Palma il Giovane), Tiziano Vecellio (Titian), the Veneto school of the 16th century and Lambert Sustris.

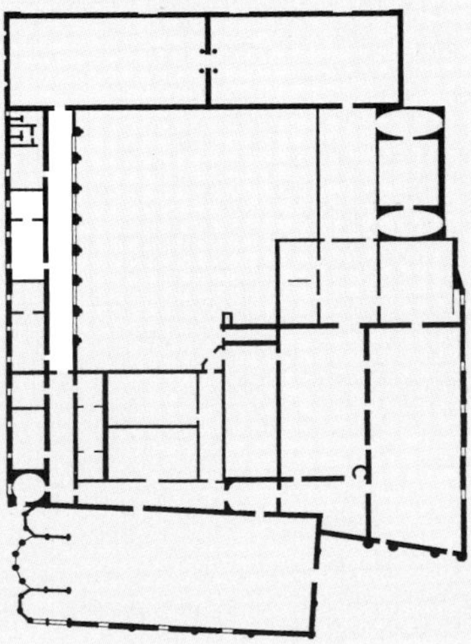

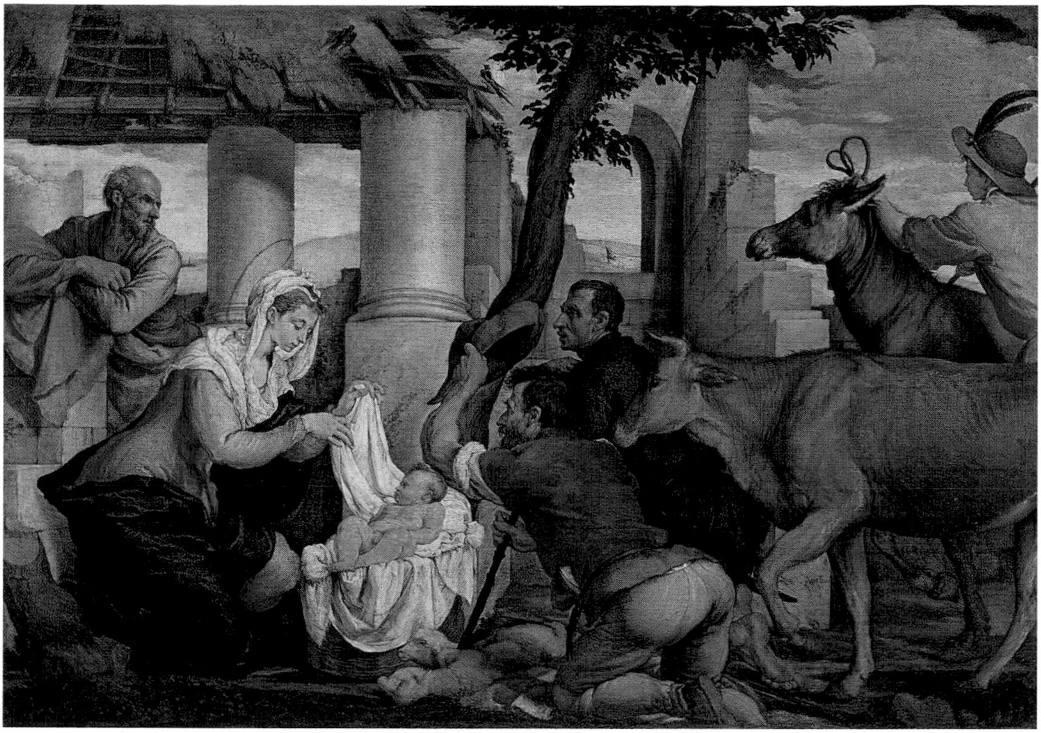

Jacopo da Ponte (Bassano)
(Bassano 1517-1592)

Adoration of the Shepherds

Canvas, cm 95 × 140
(cat. 1360)
Acquisition: 1983, by purchase.

In this composition, which evokes Titian-like themes, there is a unique blend of Parmigianino influences, Mannerist refinement and naturalistic observations. It dates to 1545 or just after.

Jacopo Robusti (Tintoretto)
(Venice 1519- 1594)

Procurator Jacopo Soranzo

Canvas, cm 106 × 90
(cat. 245)
Acquisition: 1812
Latest restoration: 1957

Dating to around 1550, this work was originally in the form of a lunette. Despite its official "formal" use, the picture, which can be dated at around 1550, reveals a surprising expressive power.

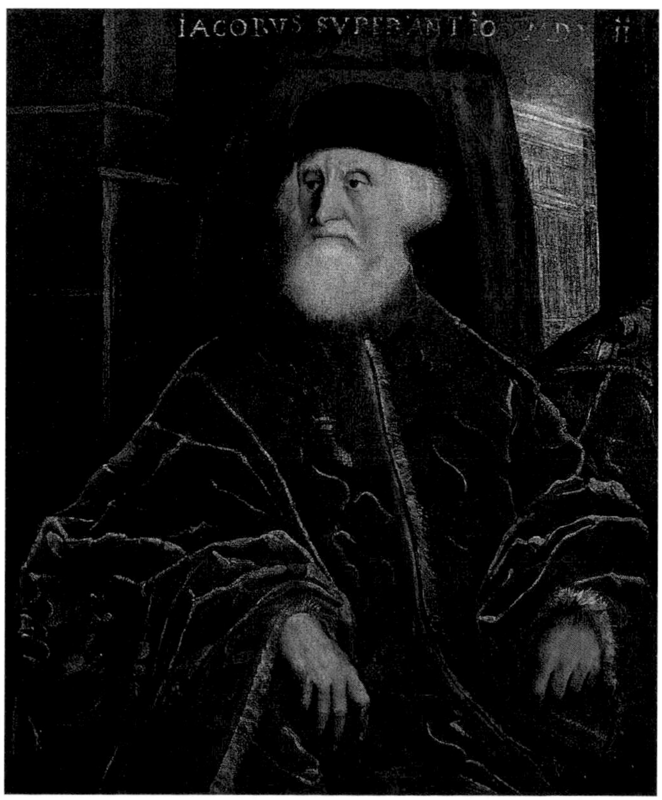

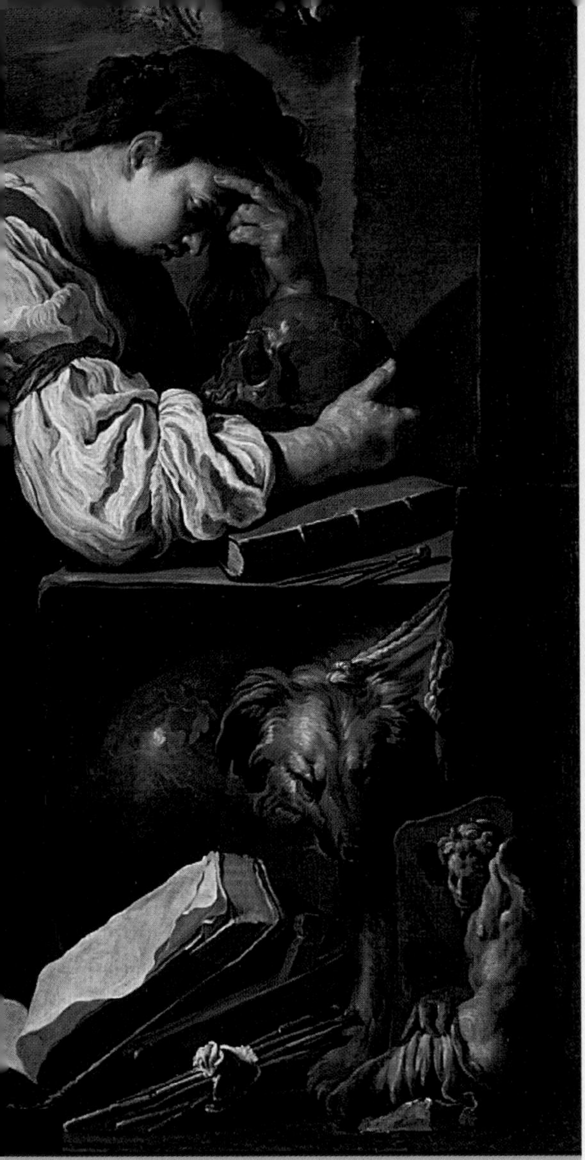

17th Century paintings

This room underwent the same changes and renovations as Room 13.
In this room are shown works by Annibale Carracci, Bernardo Strozzi, Pierfrancesco Mola, Domenico Fetti, Johann Liss, Tiberio Tinelli, an anonymous 17th-Century painter, Mattia Preti, an imitator of Giambattista Langetti, Sebastiano Mazzoni, Francesco Maffei, Pietro Muttoni (Della Vecchia) and Giulio Carpioni.

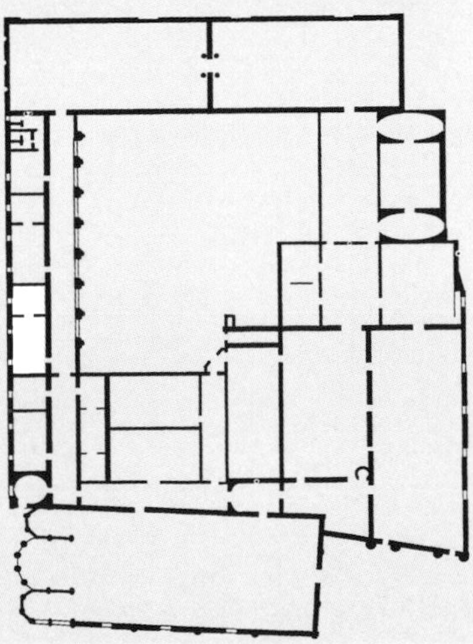

Domenico Fetti
(Rome (?) 1588/89 -Venice 1623)

David

Canvas, cm 175 × 128
(cat. 669)
Acquisition: 1838, by donation from Girolamo Contarini
Latest restoration: 1996

The painting dates from between 1617 and 1619, prior to when the artist resided in Venice. The young man, with his suffering beauty and contemporary dress recalls the Caravaggio's elegant knights.

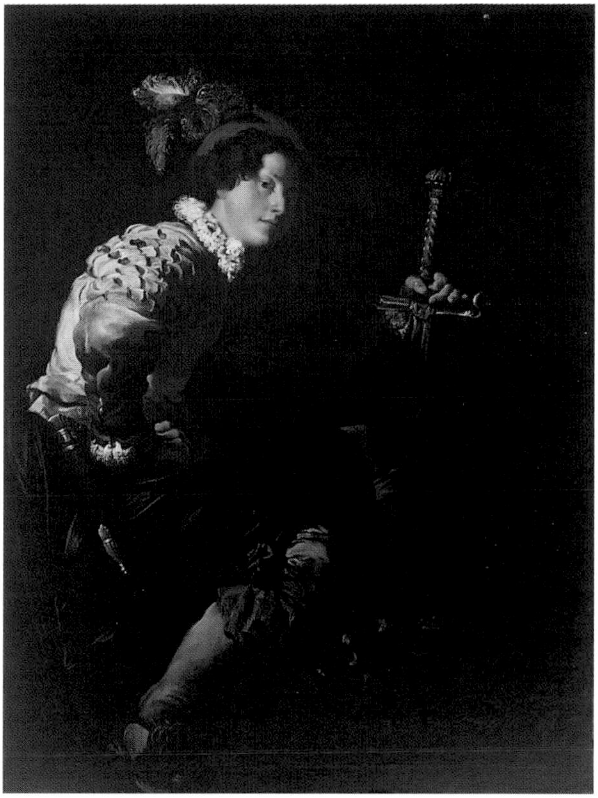

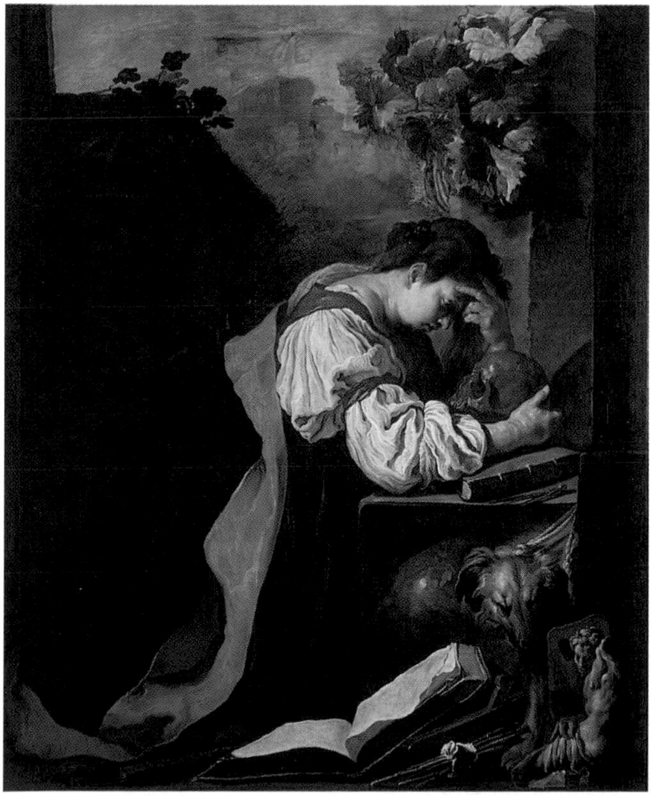

Domenico Fetti
(Rome (?) 1588/89 -Venice 1623)

Meditation

Canvas, cm 179 × 140
(cat. 671)
Acquisition: 1838, by donation from Girolamo Contarini
Latest restoration: 1961

This famous painting is believed to have been completed around 1618, before the artist resided in Venice. The female figure is situated between the still life of the lower part of the painting alluding to death and the "sadness of the world". The grapevine above symbolises life and salvation.

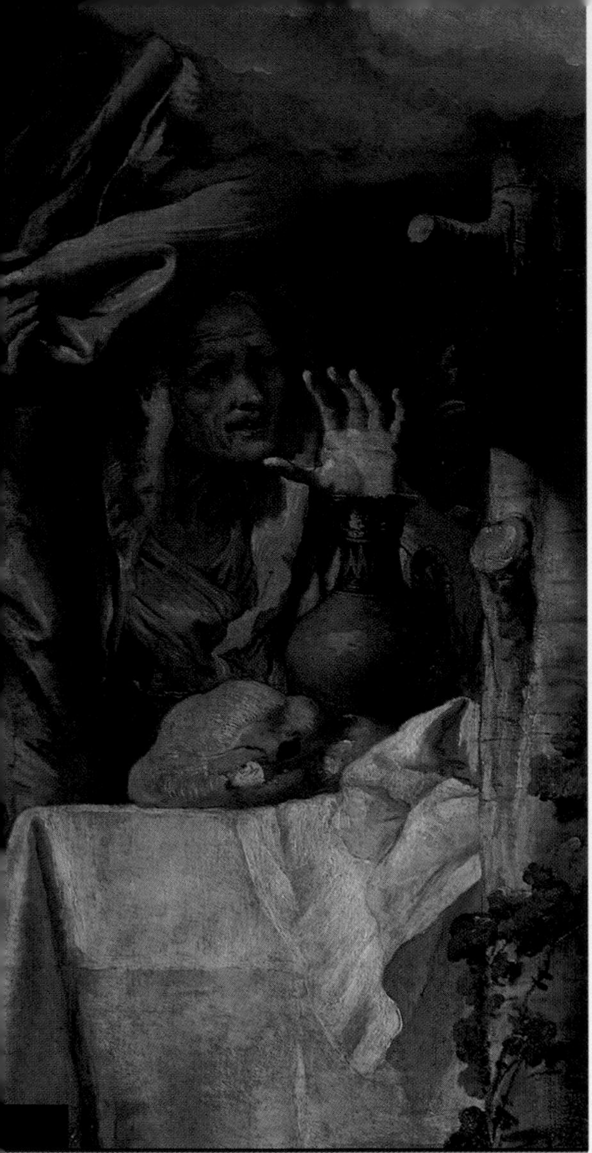

Giovanni Antonio Pellegrini, Giambattista Tiepolo and Giannantonio Guardi

This is the final part of the long Palladio corridor. The "cell" structure (rooms 16 and 16a) is to the left, while within the building itself is a large exhibition space that was created from joining three rooms (into room 17); a door remains from one of these rooms. Towards the rear, through the large doorway is found the famous oval stairway designed by Palladio in 1561.

This room displays works by Giambattista Tiepolo, Francesco Solimena, Giambattista Pittoni, Giannantonio Guardi, Giovan Antonio Pellegrini, Angelo Trevisani and Giandomenico Tiepolo.

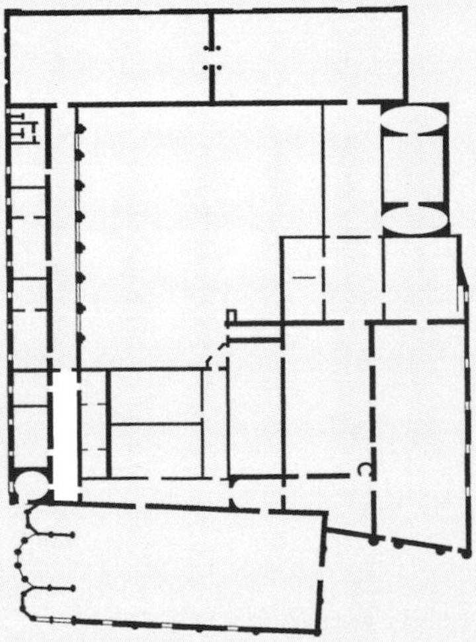

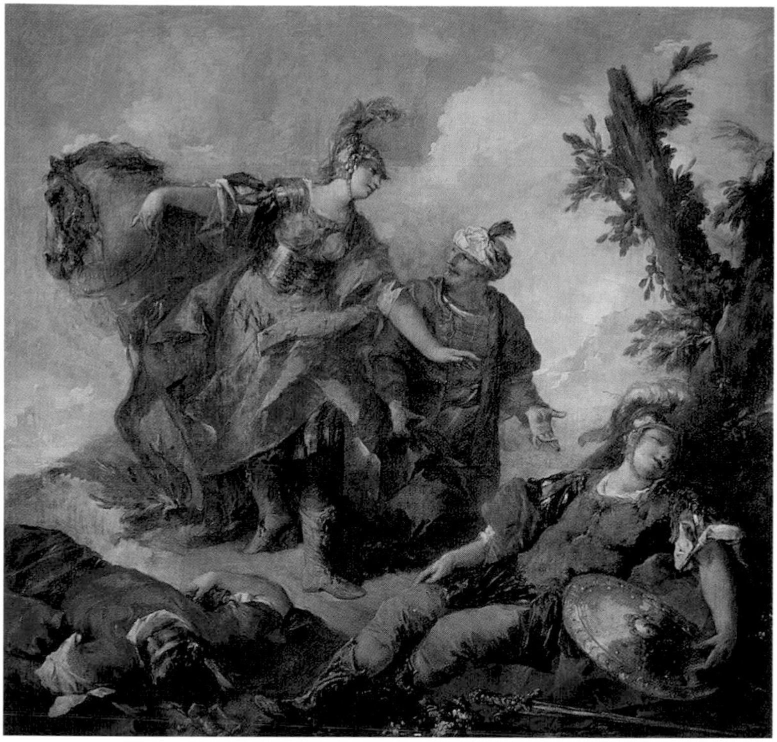

Giannantonio Guardi
(Vienna 1699-Venice 1760)

Herminia and Vaprinus happen upon the wounded Tancredi after his duel with Argante

Canvas, cm 250 × 261
(cat. 1387)
Acquisition: 1988

This is the only work by Guardi at the Accademia, and was probably part of a cycle of 13 paintings inspired by Tasso's *Jerusalem Delivered*, with engravings by Piazzetta dated around 1750-1755, at the height of his maturity.

Giandomenico Tiepolo
(Venice 1727-1804)

Abraham and the Angels

Canvas, cm 200 × 281
(cat. 834)
Acquisition: 1807
Latest restoration: 1960

This is the last painting commissioned by the Scuola della Carità to complete the decoration of the new Chancellery which was erected in 1764. The smoothness of the colour and the cold purity of the drawing are early reflections of neoclassical thought.

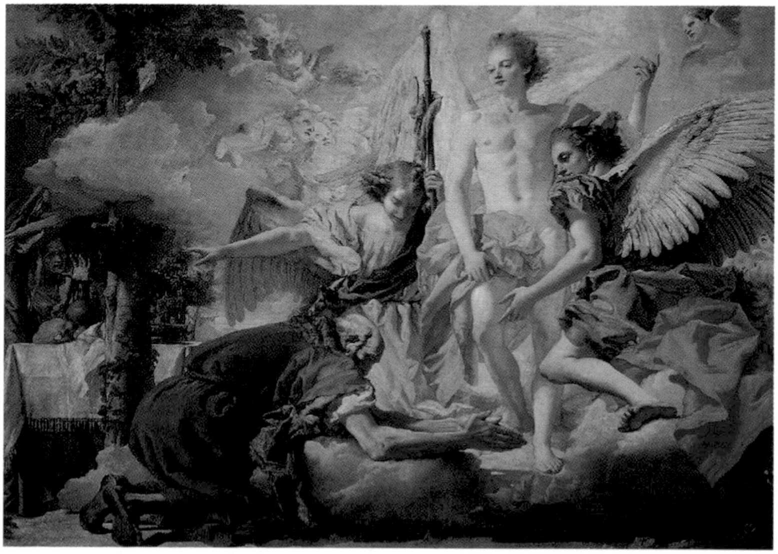

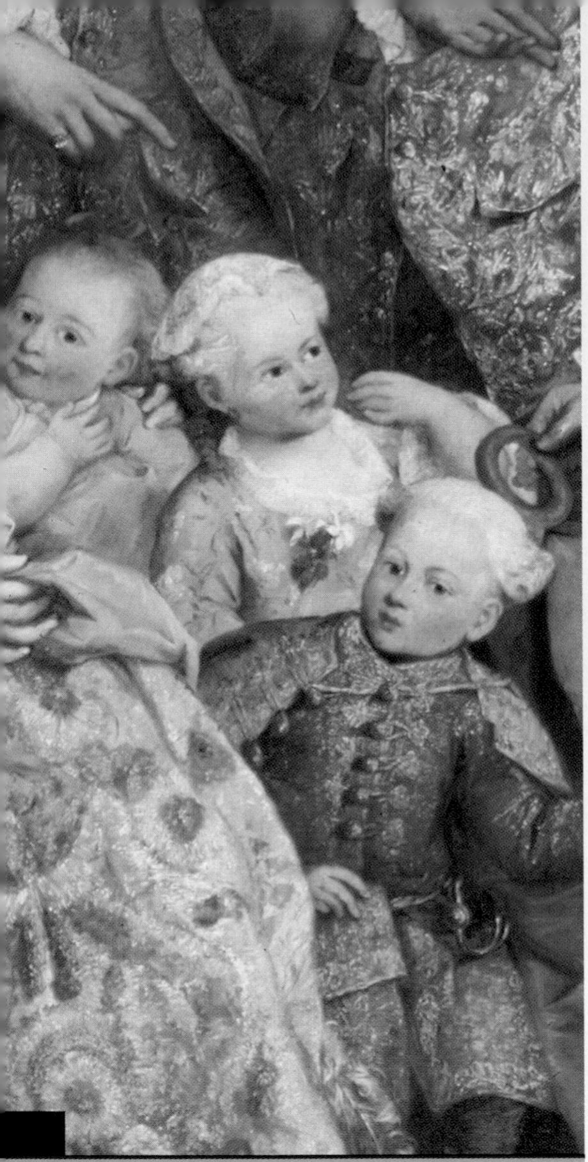

Early works by Giambattista Tiepolo, Alessandro Longhi, Giambattista Piazzetta and Fra' Galgario

The two halls maintain the original dimension of convent cell. Both were renovated in 1947 by Carlo Scarpa, who later, in 1959, went on to design the support for the *Fortune teller* by Piazzetta. The rooms also display works by Sebastiano Ricci, Giambattista Tiepolo, Gaspare Traversi, Giuseppe Angeli, Giambattista Piazzetta, Giulia Lama, Vittore Ghislandi (Fra' Galgario), Giuseppe Nogari and Alessandro Longhi.

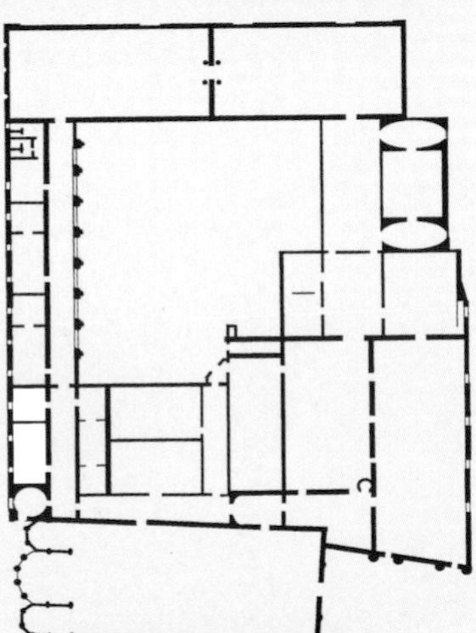

Giambattista Piazzetta
(Venice 1683-1754)

The Fortune-teller

Canvas, cm 154 × 115
(cat. 483)
Acquisition: 1887
Latest restoration: 1983

This painting, among the most famous by Piazzetta, is universally called *The Fortune-teller*, but its interpretations vary widely: it can be seen politically, symbolically or even as an amorous initiation of the two youths to the right. On the back of the original canvas is a folio with the date 1740.

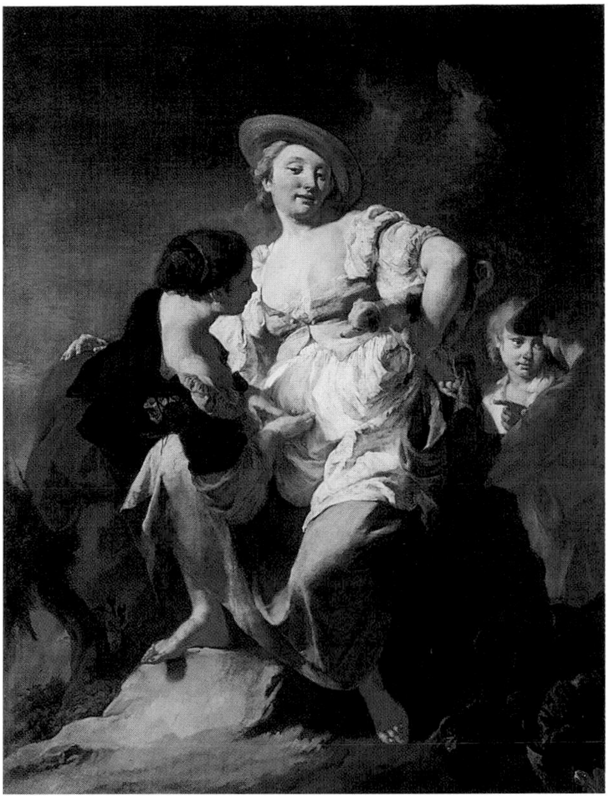

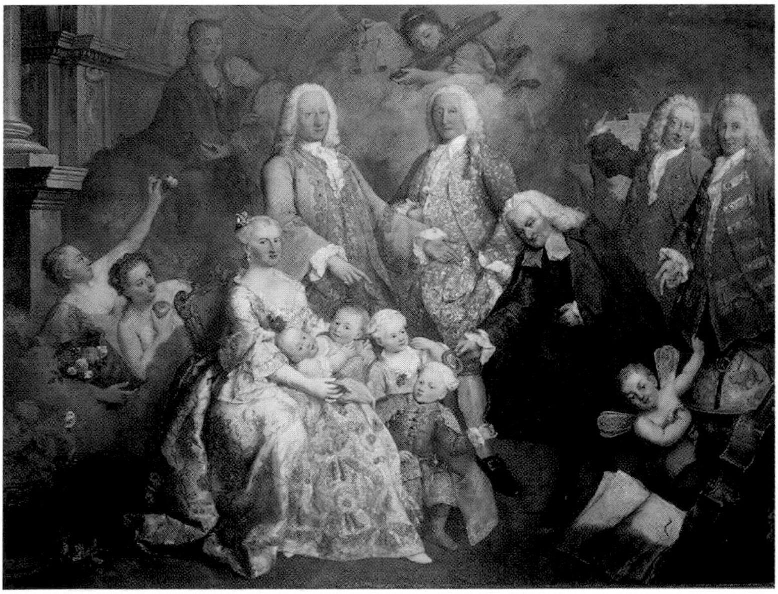

16 a

Alessandro Longhi
(Venice 1733-1813)

The Family of Procurator Luigi Pisani

Canvas, cm 255 × 340
(cat. 1355)
Acquisition: 1979, by purchase.
Latest restoration: 1996

Doge Alvise Pisani (1664-1741) is shown with his son Luigi the procurator, his wife Paolina Gambara and four children, surrounded by allegorical figures symbolising family virtues.

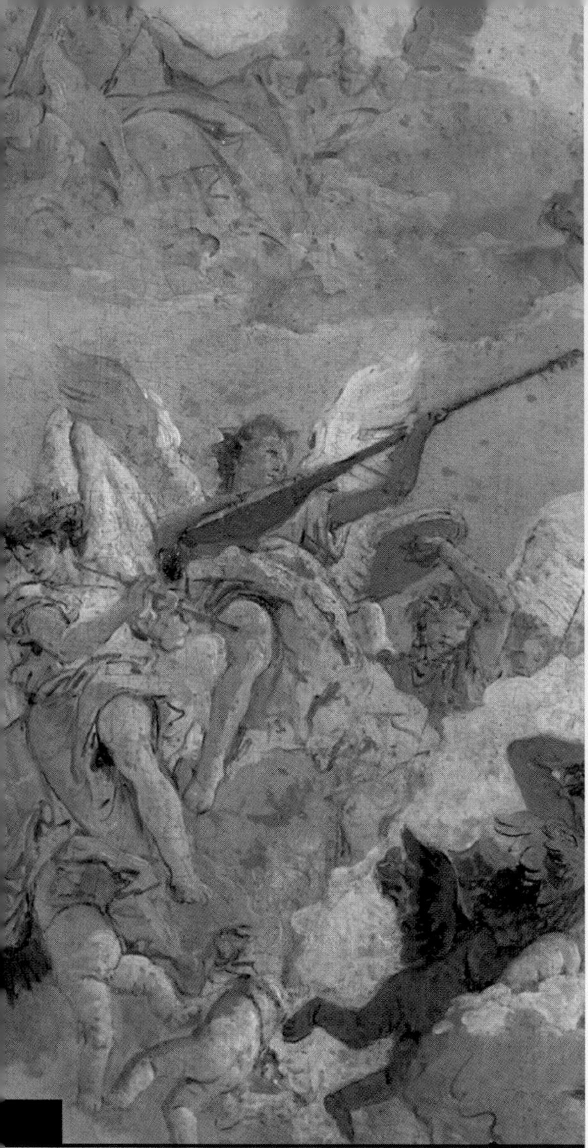

Canaletto, Francesco Guardi, Giambattista Tiepolo, Pietro Longhi, Rosalba Carriera and trial works by members of the Accademia

Room 17. This room was fitted between 1921 and 1923 for the display of small 18th-Century paintings; in 1947 Carlo Scarpa added a small narrow gallery, with a typical Venetian floor and a single velarium on the ceiling.
This room displays works by Giuseppe Zais, Bernardo Bellotto, Antonio Canal (Canaletto), Michele Marieschi, Antonio Diziani, Francesco Guardi, Marco Ricci, Giambattista Tiepolo, Jacopo Amigoni, Giambattista Pittoni, Sebastiano Ricci, Francesco Fontebasso, Alessandro Magnasco, Giambattista Piazzetta, Rosalba Carriera and Pietro Longhi.

Room 18. This hallway was constructed in the early 19th Century and redesigned by Carlo Scarpa in 1953. He closed off two windows and added a single door towards the over-hang. The wooden base was eliminated, the ceiling was lowered and new skylights were opened. The display case with the Canova sketches had been added in 1949. Originally the room was to be used for displaying a rotation of drawings, but later trial works from the old Accademia at the Fonteghetto della Farina were added.
In this room are shown works by Giuseppe Zais, Francesco Battaglioli, Giuseppe Moretti, Pietro Gaspari, Antonio Joli, Antonio Maria Visentini, Domenico Fedeli (Maggiotto), Michelangelo Morlaiter, Francesco Maggiotto, Pietro Longhi, Francesco Zuccarelli, Pierantonio Novelli, Alessandro Longhi and Antonio Canova.

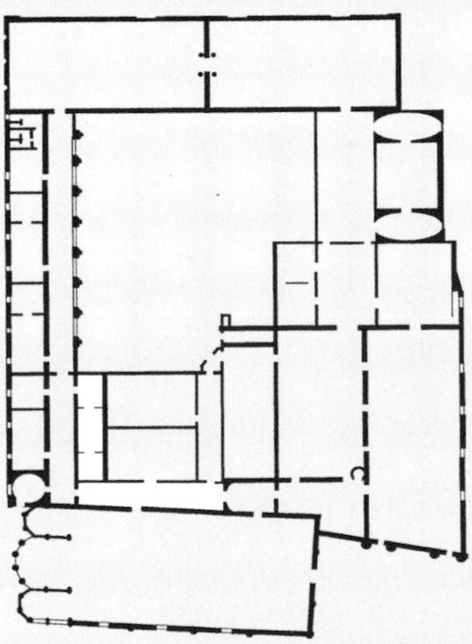

Bernardo Bellotto
(Venice 1721-Warsaw 1780)

The Scuola di San Marco

Canvas, cm 41 × 59
(cat. 494)
Acquisition: 1856, from the Manfrin collection
Latest restoration: 1990

Largely attributed to Bellotto during his apprenticeship in the studio of his uncle, Canaletto, the work dates to around 1740.

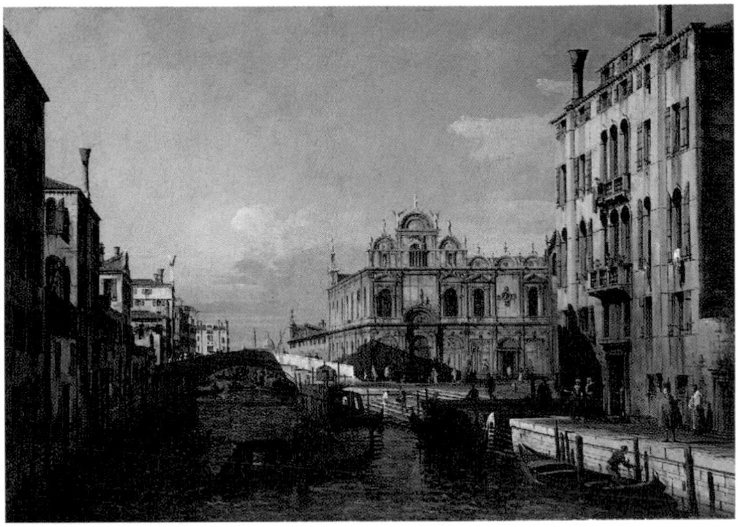

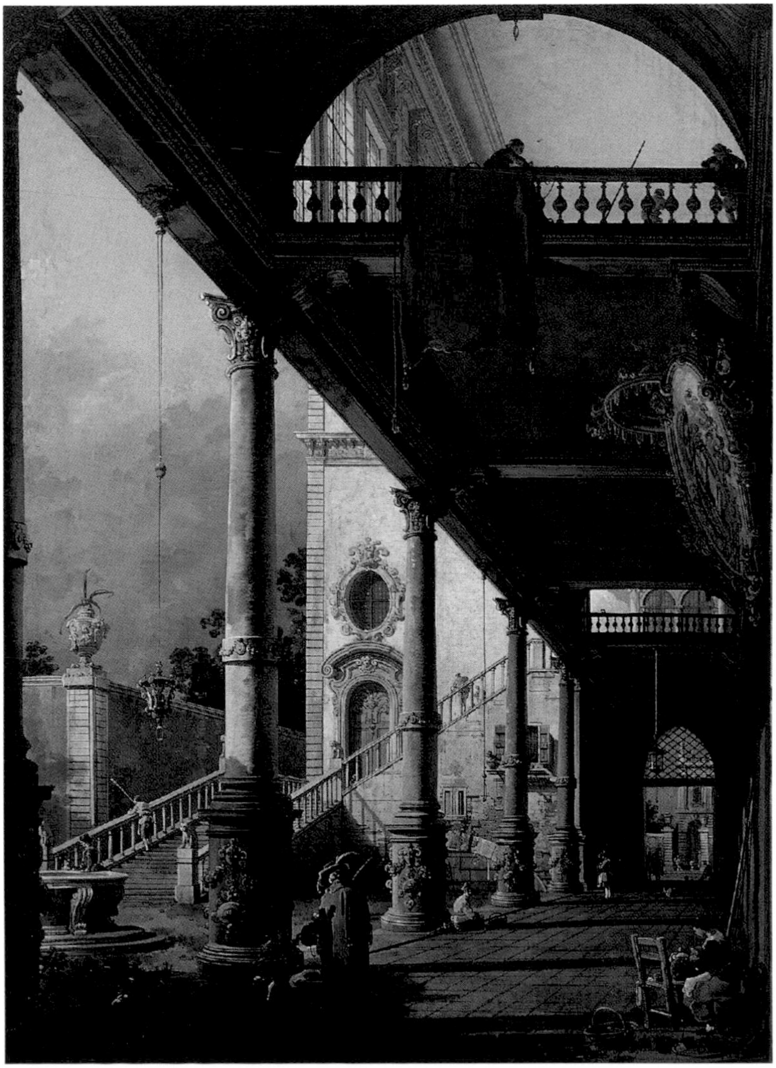

Antonio Canal (Canaletto)
(Venice 1697-1768)

Capriccio of a Colonnade

Canvas, cm 92 × 130
(cat. 463)
Acquisition: 1807
Latest restoration: 1985

17

Trial work of acceptance, after the artist was made professor of perspective architecture, signed and dated 1765. The *Capriccio* (or imaginary view), now famous, was copied many times by Canaletto himself.

Francesco Guardi
(Venice 1712-1793)

Fire at San Marcuola

Canvas, cm 32 × 51
(cat. 1344)
Acquisition: 1972, by exercise of purchase right
Latest restoration: 1993

This is Guardi's rendering of a real event: the dramatic fire at the oil storehouse in the Ghetto, which occurred on November 28, 1789. It is among the artist's masterpieces within the documentary style, composed towards his late maturity.

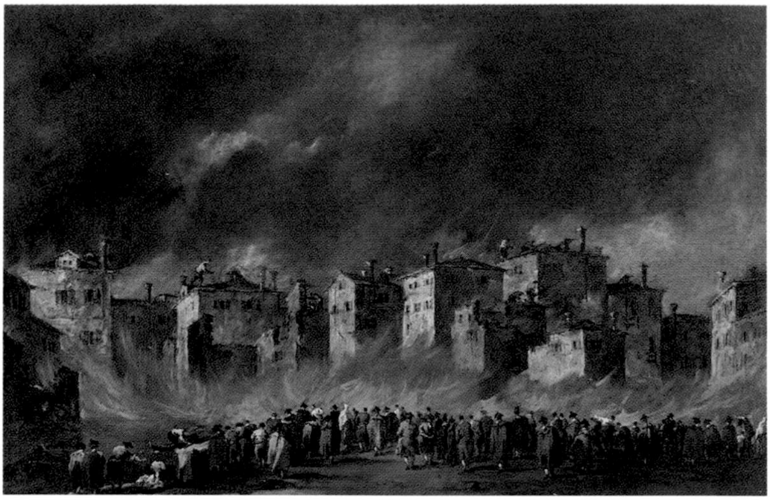

17

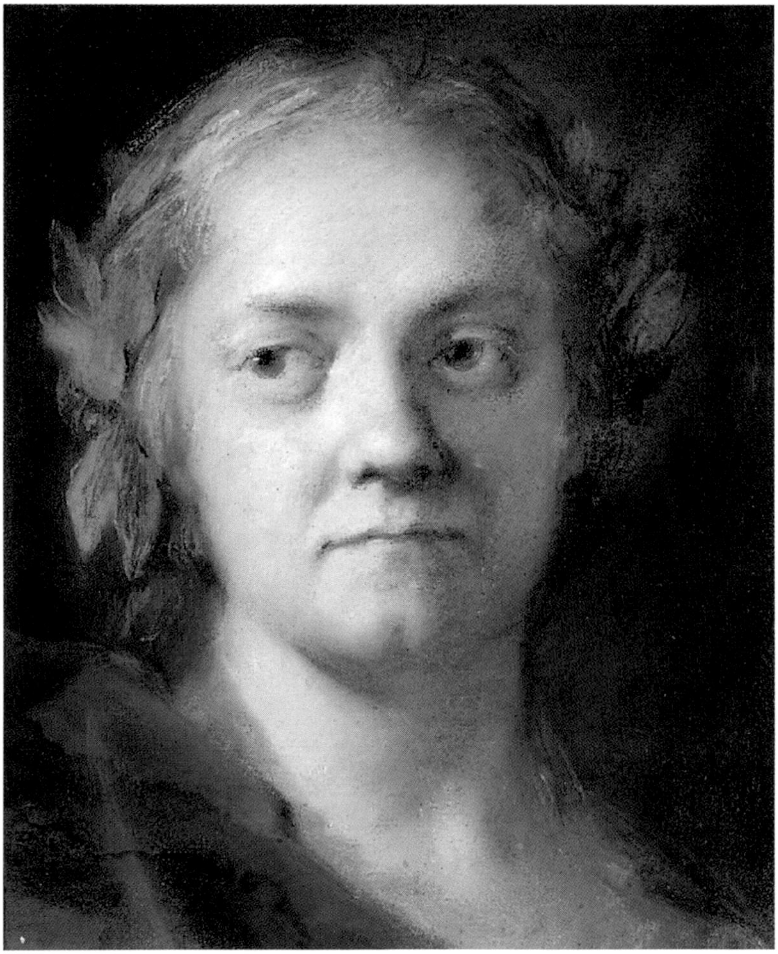

Rosalba Carriera
(Venice 1675-1758)

Self-portrait

Canvas, cm 31 × 25
(cat. 907)
Acquisition: 1927, through a purchase from the option Ditta Naya

In this painting, which was made by the artist a few years before she fell victim to "a total loss of reason", Carriera's face appears pained and tired, almost foreshadowing the real blindness that would afflict the painter in 1746.

Rosalba Carriera
(Venice 1675-1758)

Portrait of a Young Man

Canvas, cm 34 × 27
(cat. 445)
Acquisition: 1888, by bequest from Vincenzo Omoboni Astori

This work dating from 1726 is undoubtedly a portrait of the son of the French consul Le Blond, and reveals an image of exquisite grace and gentleness.

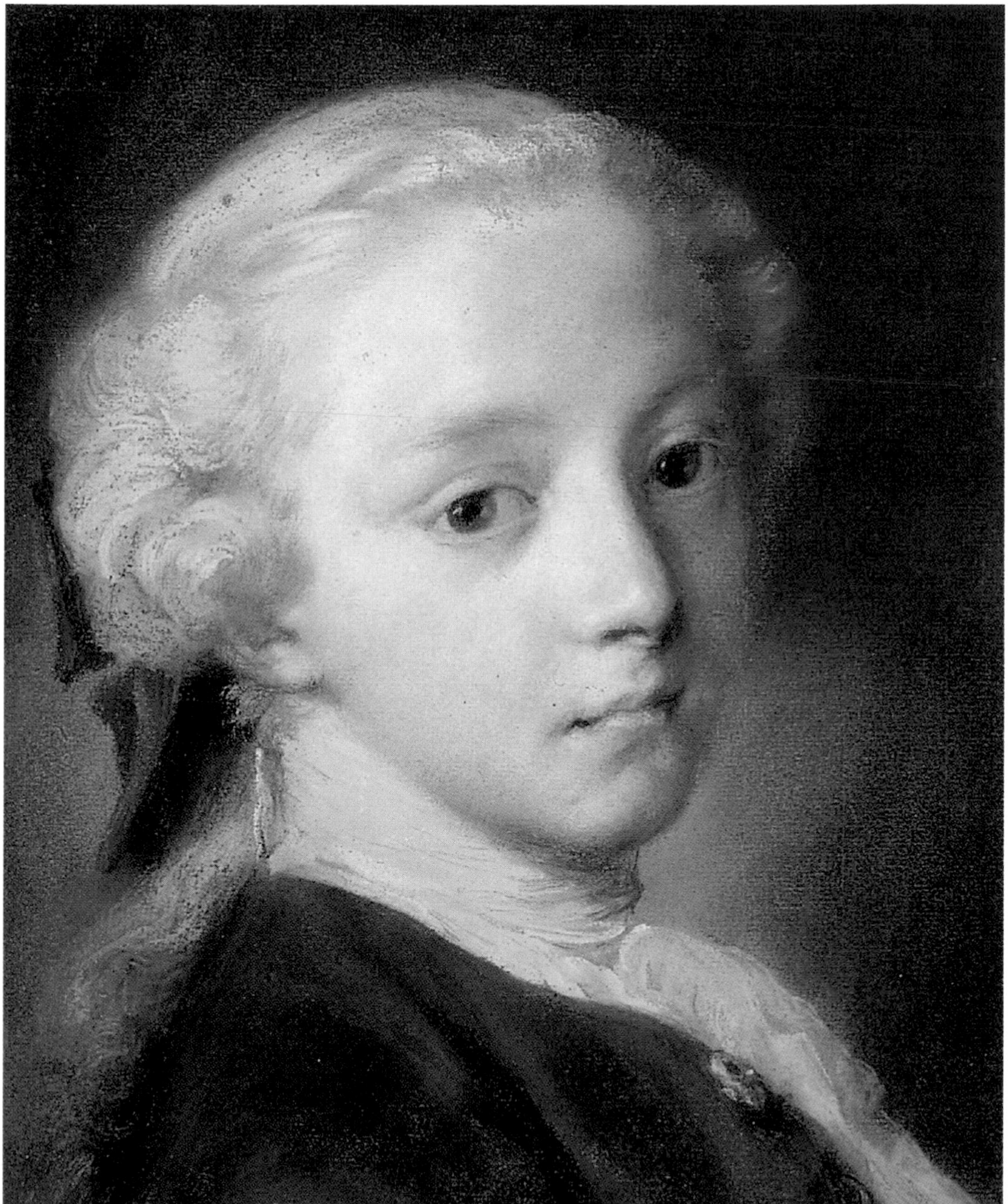

17

Francesco Guardi
(Venice 1712-1783)

St. Mark's Bassin with San Giorgio and Giudecca

Canvas, cm 69 × 94
(cat. 709)
Acquisition: 1903, donation by John of Lichtenstein
Latest restoration: 1993

On the house at bottom left the initials F.G. It is one of the many versions of a theme the artist often painted. To the left the island of San Giorgio Maggiore, to the right Giudecca with the now-destroyed church of San Giovanni Battista. The painting should not be dated later than 1774, the year in which the bell-tower in San Giorgio suddenly collapsed; we see it here with its original "onion" cupola.

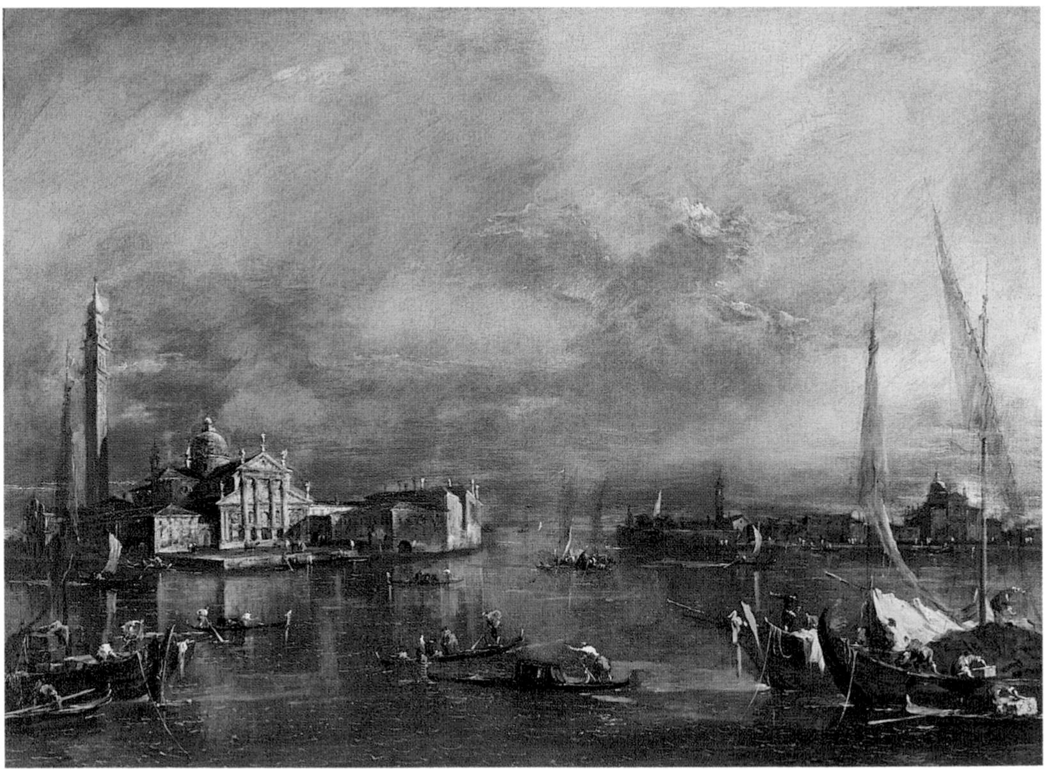

17

Pietro Longhi
(Venice 1701-1785)
The Apothecary
Canvas, cm 59 × 48
(cat. 467)
Acquisition: 1835, by donation from Girolamo Contarini.

With the artist's signature on the back, this is probably his most famous painting. The interior evokes with extraordinary success an 18th-Century apothecary shop.

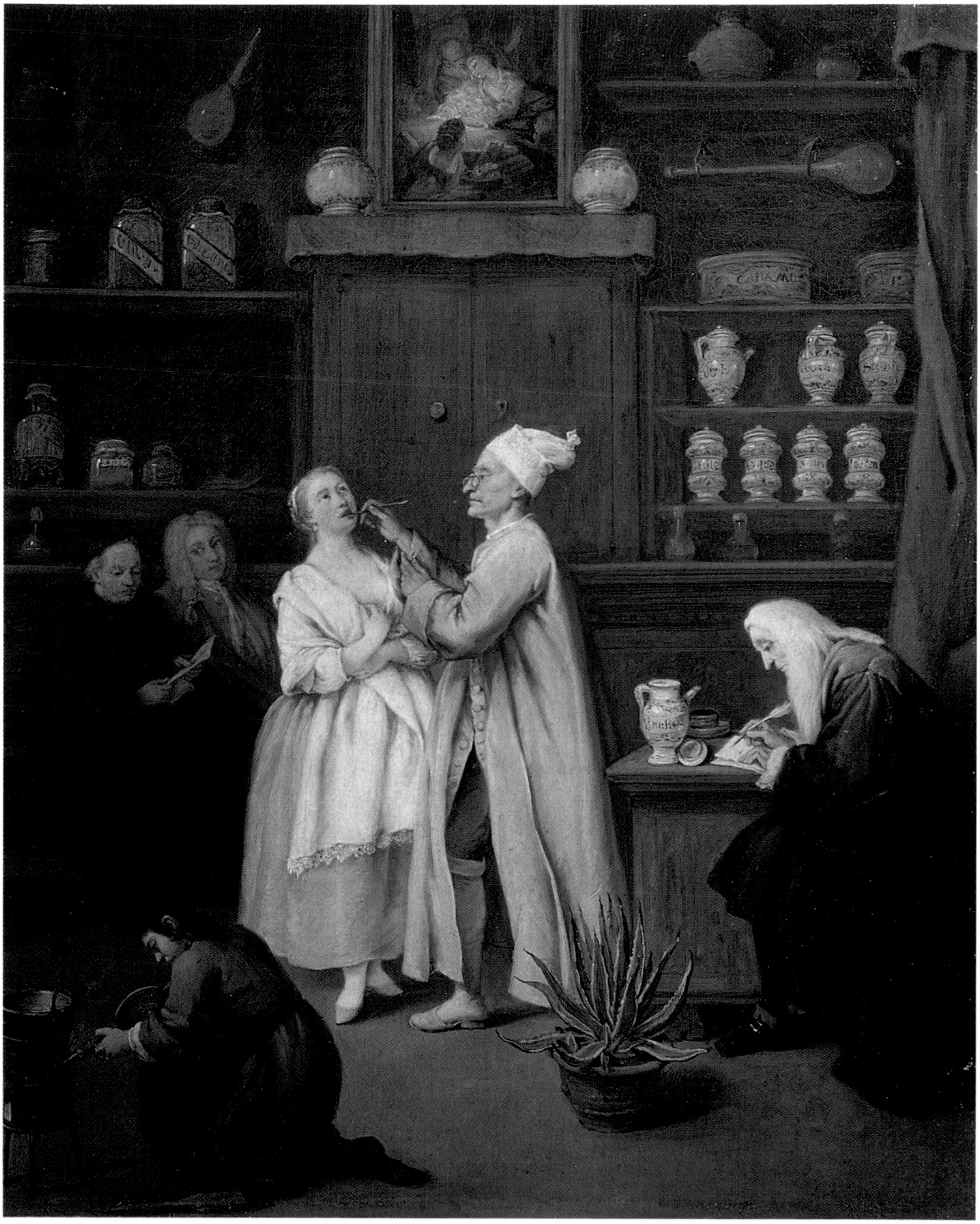

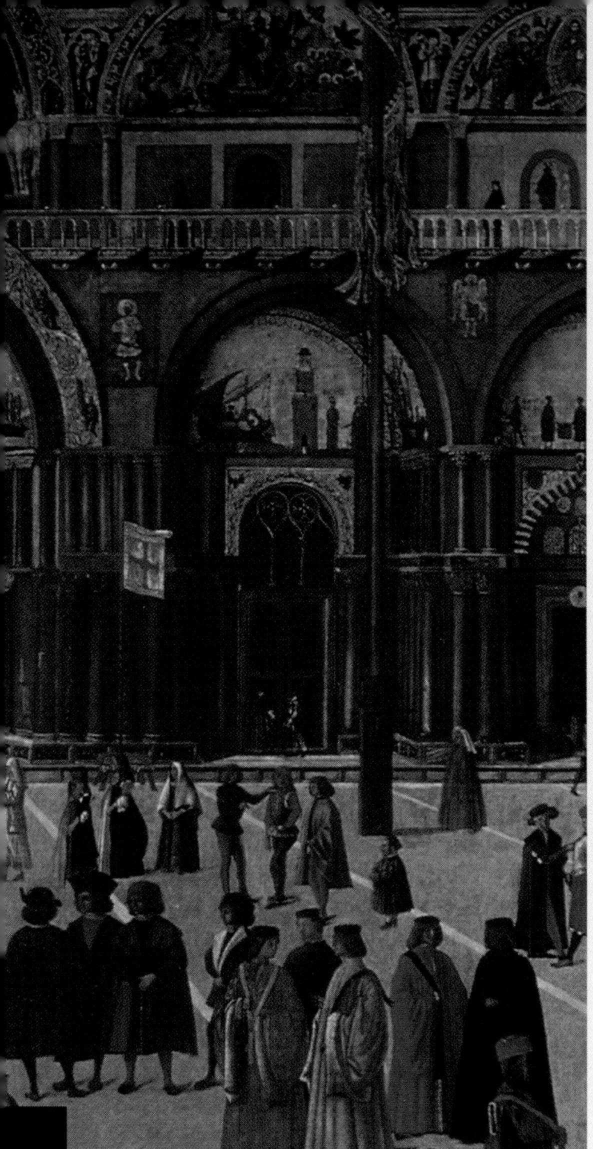

Bartolomeo Montagna, Giovanni Agostino da Lodi, Boccaccio Boccaccino and "Stories of the Relic of the Cross"

Room 19. This is a corridor which connects with rooms 20 and 21, showing 15th-Century "story" cycles. The platform at the back with the sash window from which one can admire the view of the Palladio convent, was designed by Carlo Scarpa in 1947.
In this room are shown works by Giovanni Agostino da Lodi, Pietro de Saliba, Antonello de Saliba, Marco Basaiti, Bartolomeo Cincani (il Montagna), Jacopo Parisati (da Montagnana), Boccaccio Boccaccino, Marco Marziale and an anonymous Veneto painter from the early 16th Century.

Room 20. This room was already constructed in 1940. Seven years later the canvases with the "Miracles of the Cross" were placed here provisionally; in 1959-1960 Carlo Scarpa completed the arrangement. The cycle originally served to adorn the walls of the Albergo Room or the Cross Room in the Scuola di San Giovanni Evangelista, where there is still a relic of the Holy Cross on display, donated to the guild in 1369 by Philippe de Mezióres, the Great Chancellor of the kingdom of Cyprus. There were originally ten canvases, including *The Miracle of the Vendramin Ships* by Pietro Perugino, completed in 1494. Unfortunately only eight are on display at the Accademia; Perugino's canvas – composed while he was in Venice working in the Doge's Palace – was destroyed and replaced in 1588.
The Scuola di San Giovanni Evangelista was suppressed by Napoleonic decree in 1806, and the paintings were delivered to the Accademia in 1820; they were displayed separately at various times until they were finally consolidated in 1947.
In this room are shown works by Vittore Carpaccio, Giovanni Mansueti, Gentile Bellini, Benedetto Rusconi (Diana), Lazzaro Bastiani and Giovanni Mansueti.

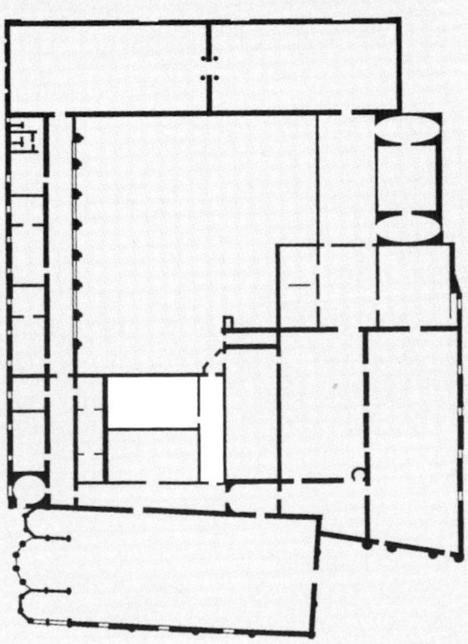

Vittore Carpaccio
(1460 ca.-1526)

Miracle of the Cross at the Rialto

Canvas, cm 371 × 392
(cat. 566)
Acquisition: 1820
Latest restoration: 1990-91

This canvas, completed in 1494, narrates the miraculous healing of a possessed man. The artist synthesises three fundamental moments: the procession on the bridge, the entrance of the patriarch, and the miracle which takes place on the loggia. But even this event is overshadowed by the representation of the city itself.

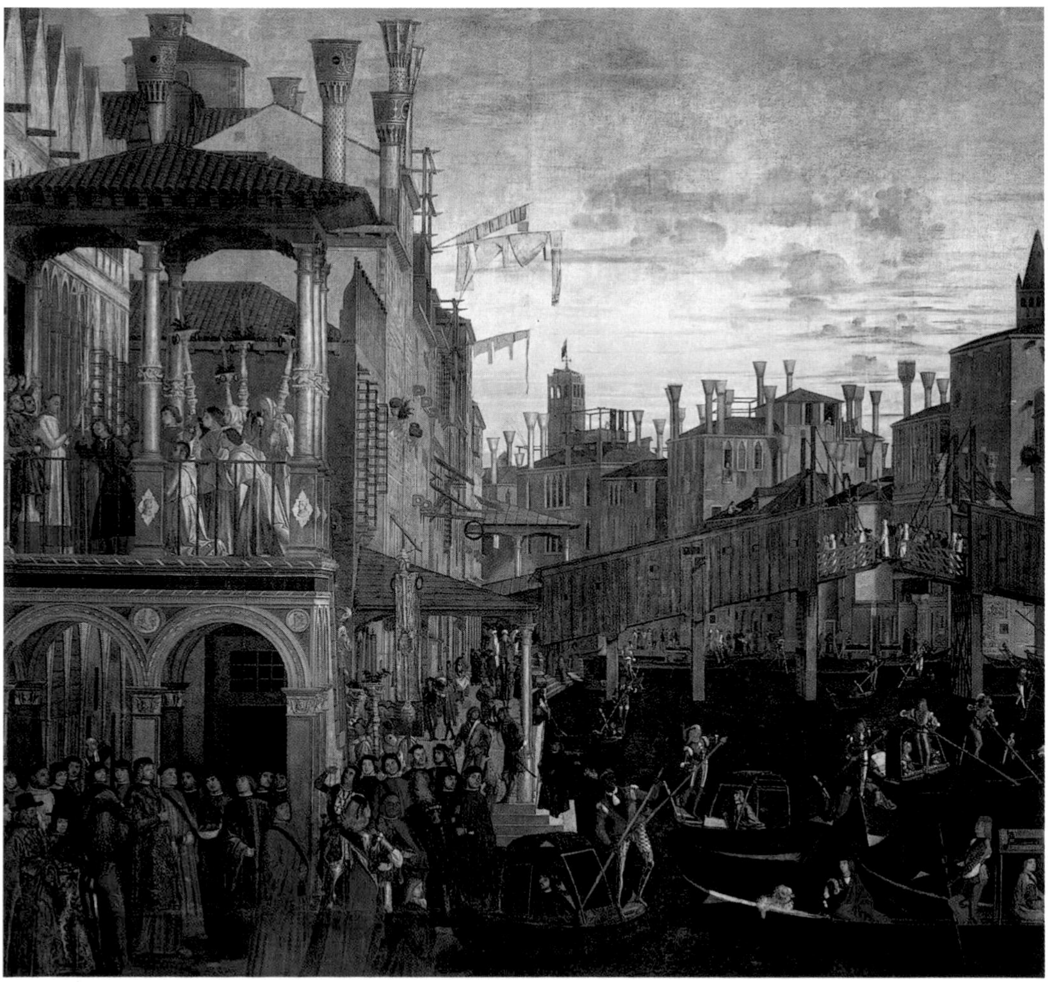

20

Gentile Bellini
(Venice 1429-1507)

Procession in Piazza San Marco

Canvas, cm 373 × 745
(cat. 567)
Acquisition: 1820
Latest restoration: 1988-89

At the bottom in the centre of the painting can be read the date 1496 and the artist's signature. The painting depicts the procession taking place in Piazza San Marco on the Feast of Saint Mark. All the schools participated in this event with their respective relics. The procession is described with less attention than the square itself, however, which is shown here as it appeared before the changes made to it in the 16th Century.

20

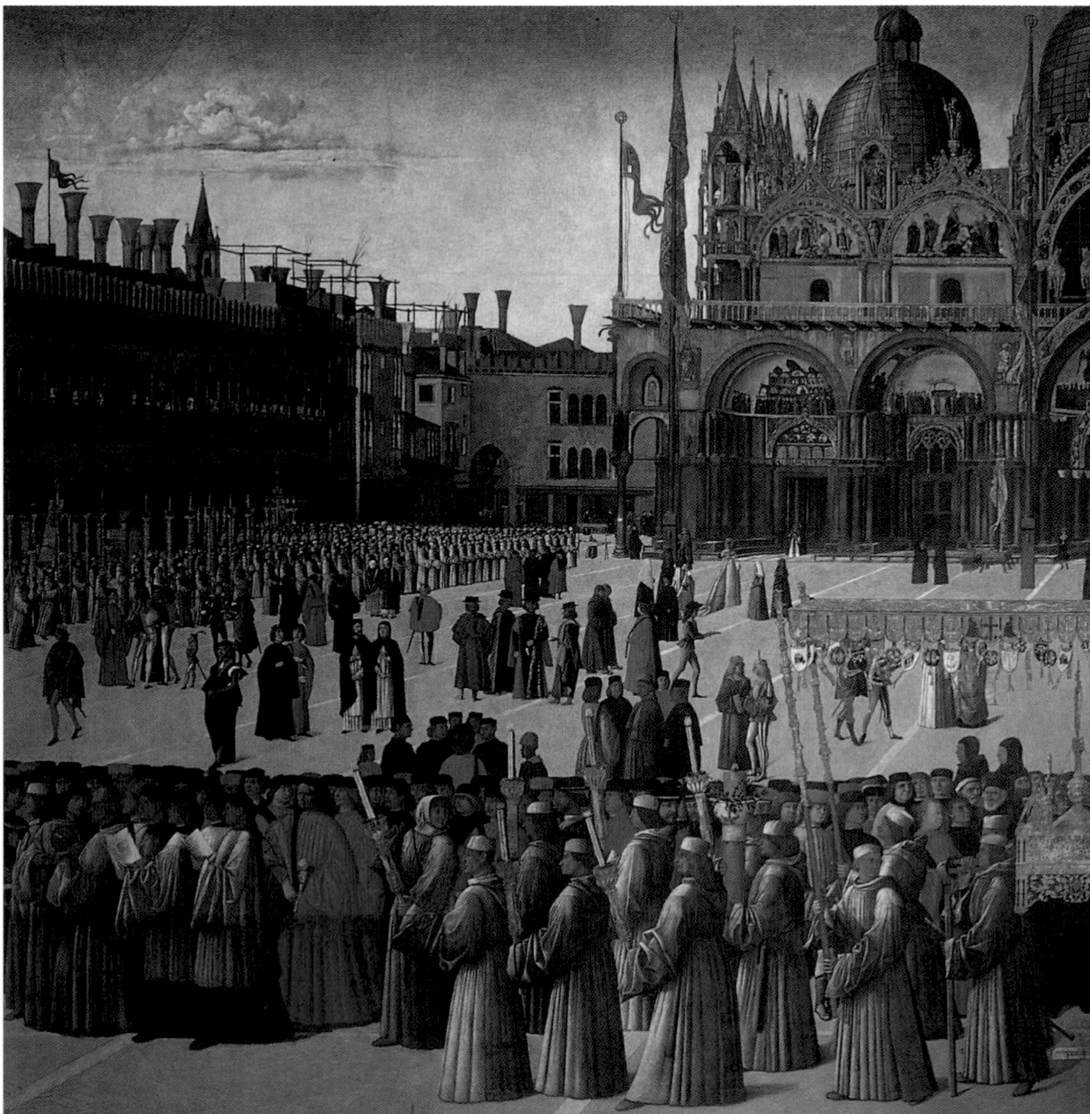

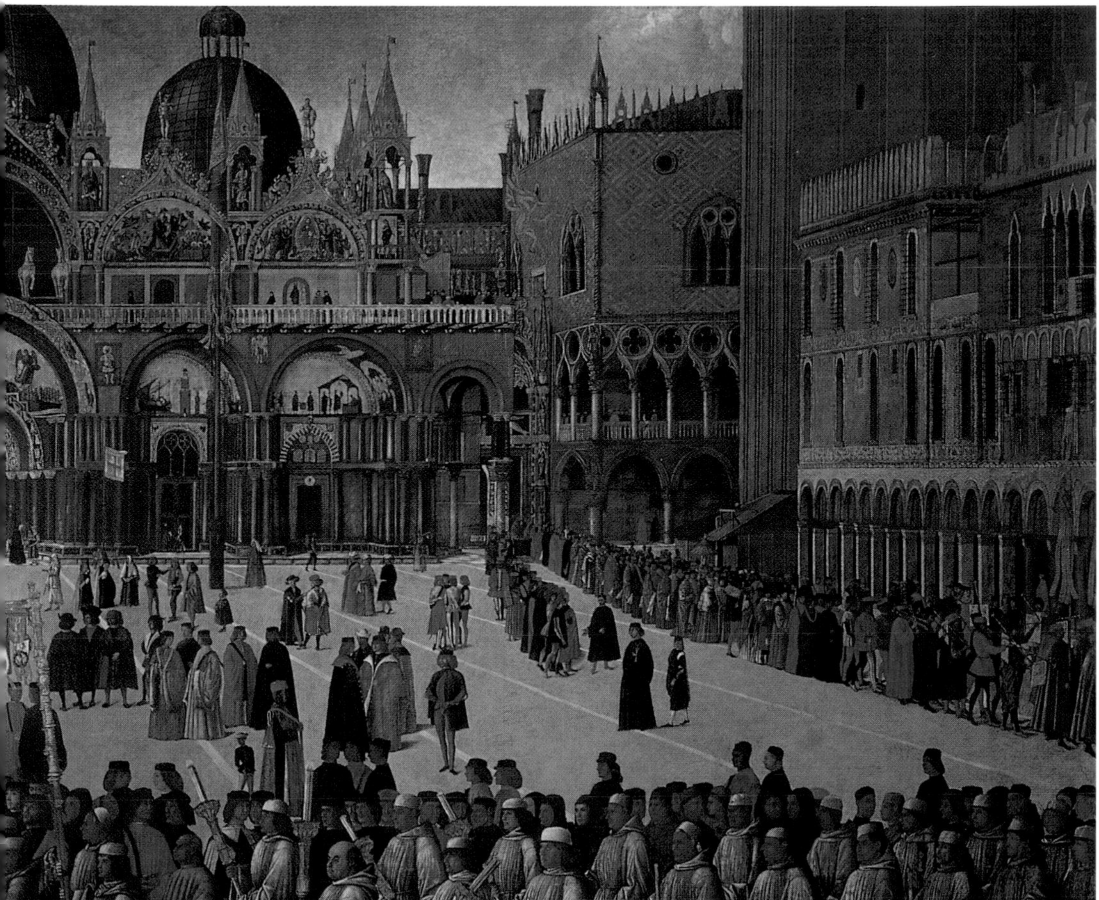

20

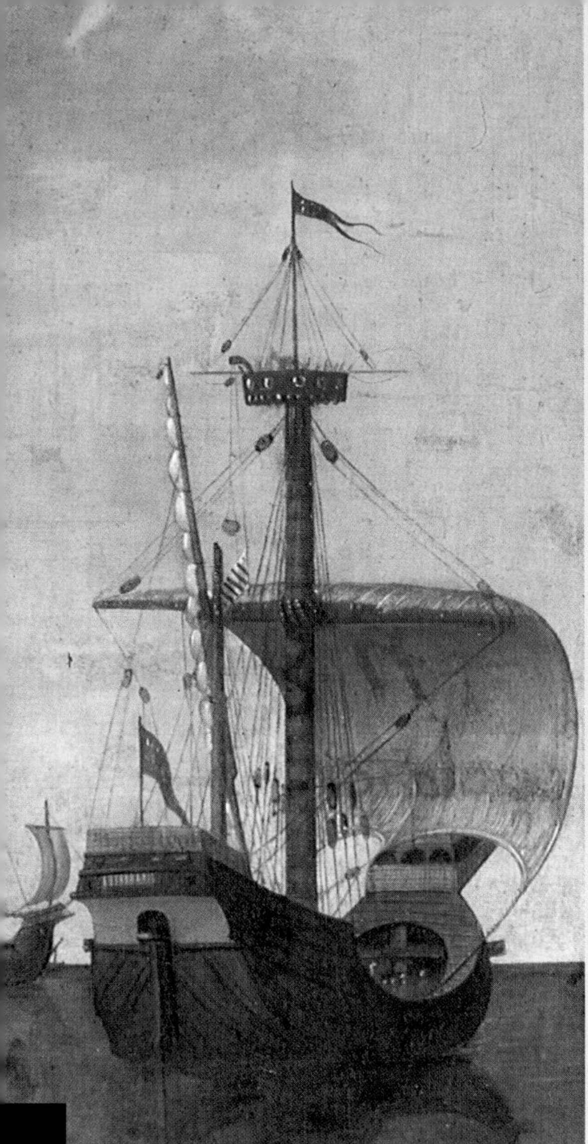

Vittore Carpaccio's "Saint Ursula" Cycle and Neoclassical Hallway

Room 21. In this room, which once held the collection of Girolamo Contarini, the "Saint Ursula" Cycle by Carpaccio was installed between 1921 and 1923. From 1959-1960 Carlo Scarpa remodelled the room, lowering the paintings, which were held up and surrounded by a strip of light oak with a subtle gilt border.
The altarpiece, set slightly back and illuminated from the side by a new source of light, was separated from the canvases with wooden screens. The works come from the Scuola di Sant'Orsola – today the canonry of the church of Santi Giovanni e Paolo, which had decided in 1488 to decorate its site with "the stories of Madonna Saint Ursula". Carpaccio composed nine paintings dating from 1490 to 1495. The stylistic differences of the canvases – which have also undergone numerous restorations and changes – are attributed to the many assistants. In fact, the artist made wide use of preparatory cartoons which were placed on the canvas using the dusting system – a task partly shared by various assistants. Based on an affirmation in *De origine, situ urbis Venetie* by Marin Sanudo, who noted in 1493 that "...among the interesting things of this city is the chapel of Saint Ursula at San Zuanne Polo, and the beautiful figures and stories in it", it is

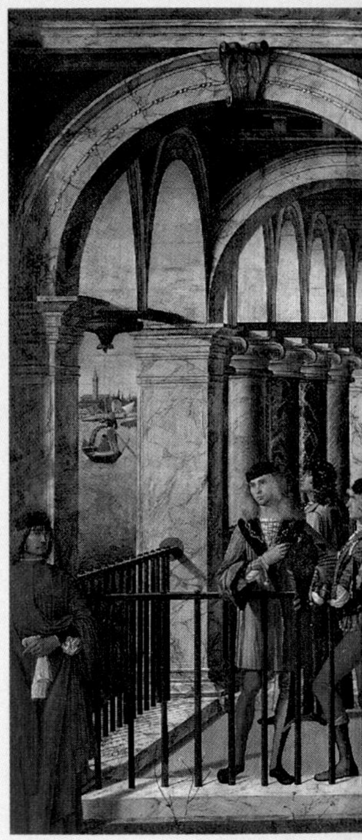

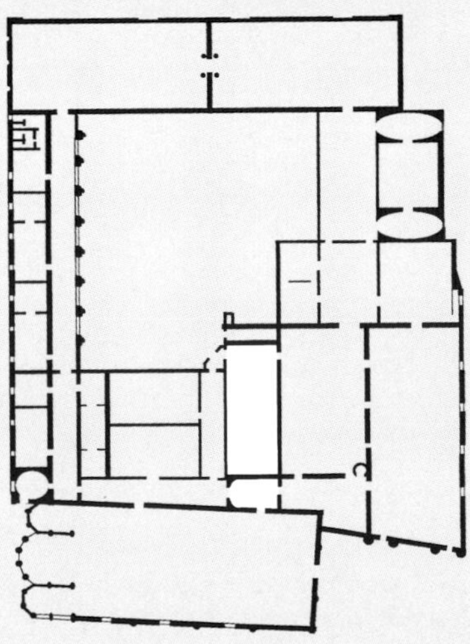

likely that most of the cycle had been completed by that time. The cycle narrates the story of Ursula, taken rather liberally from the *Legenda Aurea*, written by Jacopo da Varagine in 1475: Ursula, the Christian Briton princess, agrees to marry the Prince Hereus of England, provided that he is baptised. Together they go on a pilgrimage to Rome and many young women accompany them. They arrive in Cologne with the Pope himself and are slain by the Huns – an event that had been foretold to Ursula in a dream.

Room 22. The plan of this small circular room that leads into the Albergo Room was overseen by Francesco Lazzari between 1821 and 1823, who decorated and adorned it with sculptures and bas reliefs by Canova-influenced artists.
In this room are shown works by Rinaldo Rinaldi, Antonio Giaccarelli and Jacopo De Martini.

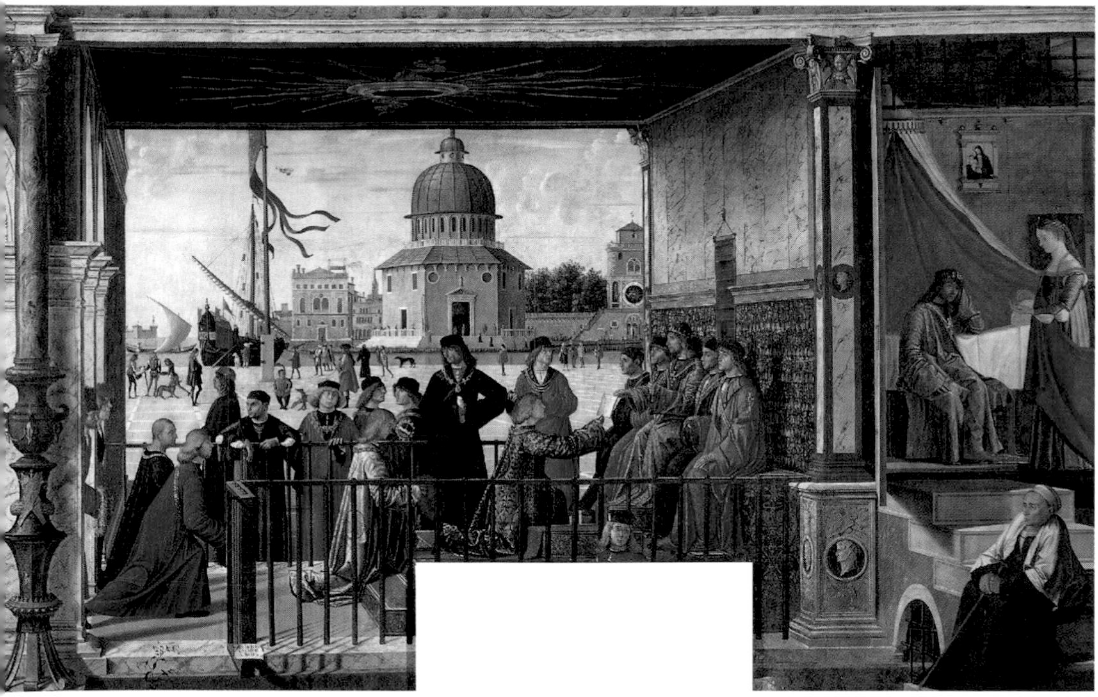

Vittore Carpaccio
(c. 1460-1526)
The Arrival of the Ambassadors
Canvas, cm 278 × 589
(cat. 572)
Acquisition: 1812
Latest restoration: 1983

This canvas incorporates three separate scenes, set off by three architectural elements: the arrival of the ambassadors at the court of Britain; the presentation of Prince Hereus's marriage proposal; Ursula in her room relates to her father the marriage conditions she requires while the nurse waits at the foot of the stairs. The building in the centre is inspired by the Temple of Jerusalem.

Vittore Carpaccio
(c. 1460-1526)

Meeting and Departure of the Betrothed

Canvas, cm 279 × 610
(cat. 575)
Acquisition: 1812
Latest restoration: 1983-84

This canvas is divided into four episodes: the prince takes leave of his parents before departing; the betrothed meet; the two betrothed bid farewell to the king and queen, and lastly they set sail on the ships which will bring them to Rome. In the background are shown the locations of the story: on the left Medieval England, on the right Renaissance Britain.

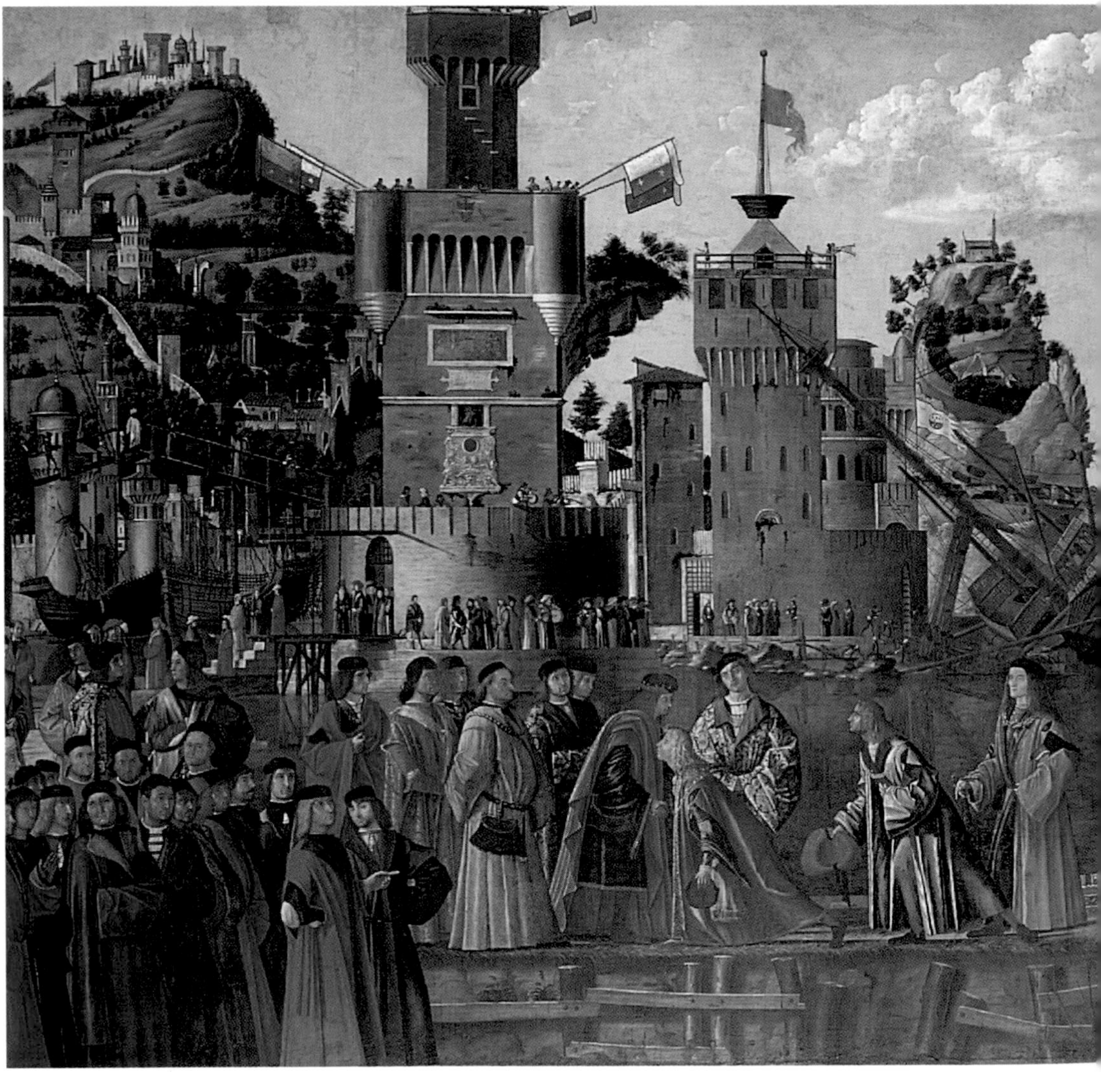

21

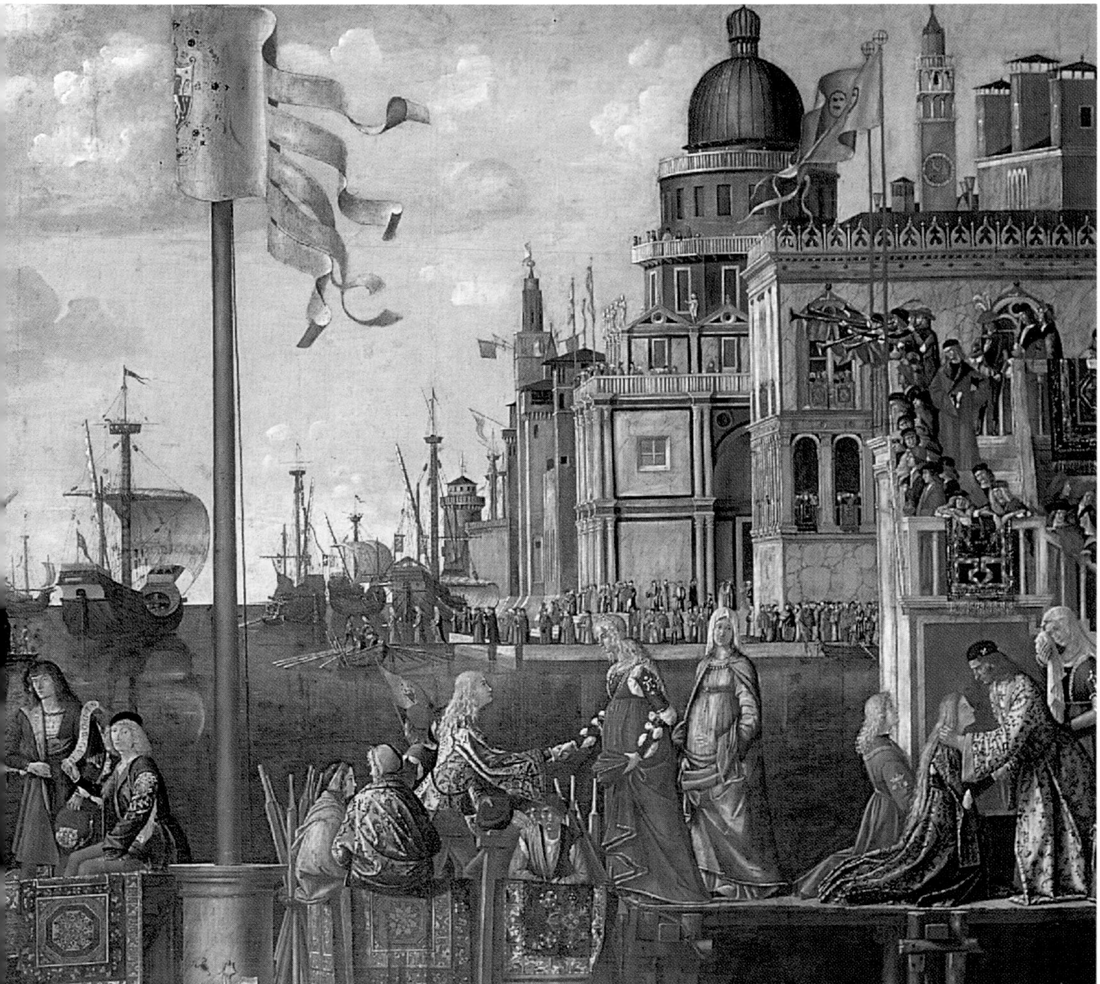

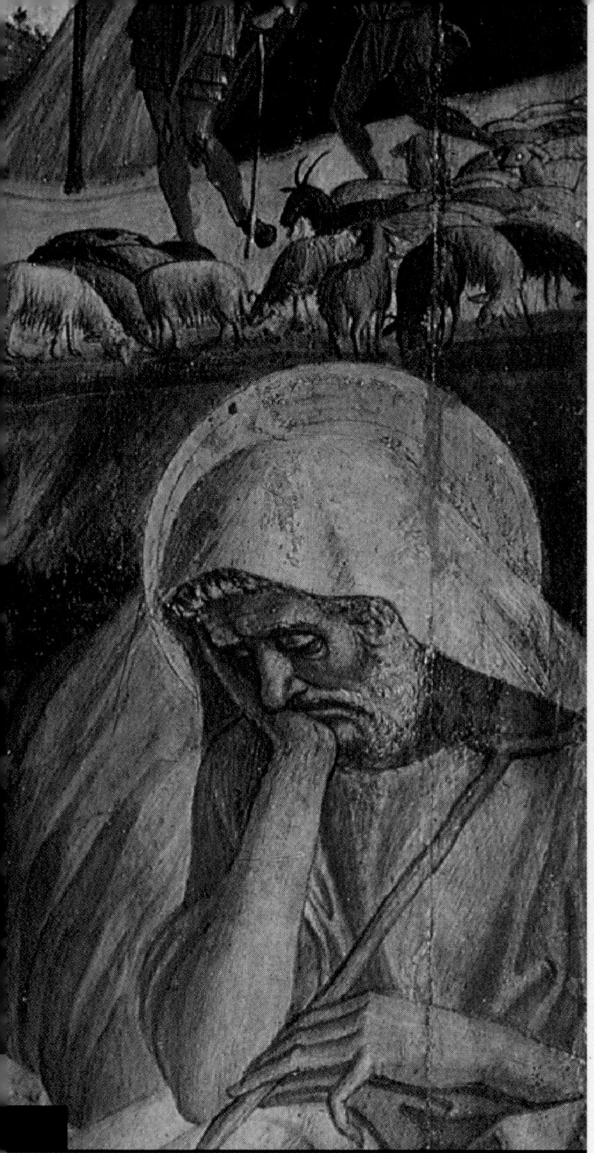

Former Church of Santa Maria della Carità. Works from the Veneto school of the 15th Century, and canvases from the Scuola di San Marco

The founding of the church of Santa Maria della Carità, which probably occurred at the beginning of the 12th Century, is part history, part myth. According to Sansovino (1581), it was originally a small wooden building "... around a capital of an image of the Virgin, famous for various miracles." Only later was it decided to construct a church in stone on the site. In 1134 some Augustinian monks from Santa Maria in Porto relocated from Ravenna to Venice and built their convent next to the church of Santa Maria della Carità. According to legend, in 1177 Pope Alexander III – in order to escape from Frederick Barbarossa – hid in the convent for six months and consecrated the church on April 5. From then on, every year on that date the Doge and Venetians of every class – even the inhabitants of the provinces – came to the church of Santa Maria della Carità to obtain the papal indulgence he had granted for the help received. Crossing the Grand Canal to the church was made easier by the construction of a bridge of boats from Campo San Vidal to Campo Santa Maria della Carità. This custom lasted until the end of the Republic. The old façade of the church can be seen in a painting kept in Room 24, which illustrates the meeting of the doge and the pope. From archival documents we know that at the end of the 13th Century the church had an external portico – once very common on Venetian buildings – of which there are now only two examples remaining: one at San Giacomo di Rialto and another at San Nicolò dei Mendicoli. There was also a bell tower for this original structure, which was left intact even during the modifications made in the 15th Century, until on March 17, 1744, when, due to the erosion at its base, it finally succumbed and toppled into the Grand Canal. There were many illustrious figures buried there as we can deduce from the register published by Tassini in 1876; a part of

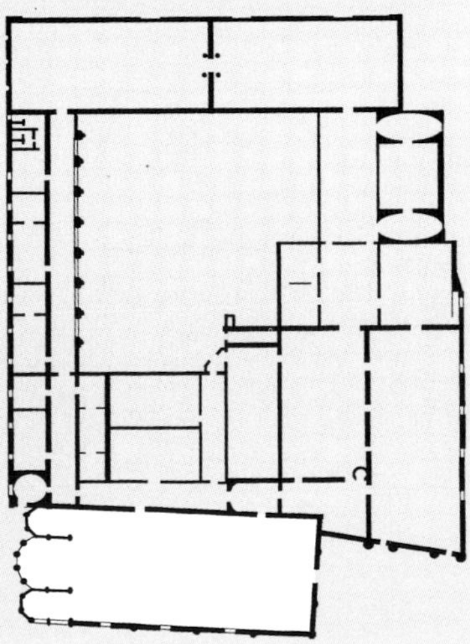

Maestro della Madonna del Parto

The Madonna del Parto and two Devouts

Panel, cm 188 × 138 (cat. 1328)
Acquisition: 1916
Latest restoration: 1996

On the open book is an invocation to the Virgin Mary, Madonna del Parto. The work is from the late 14th Century and comes from the church of Santa Caterina.

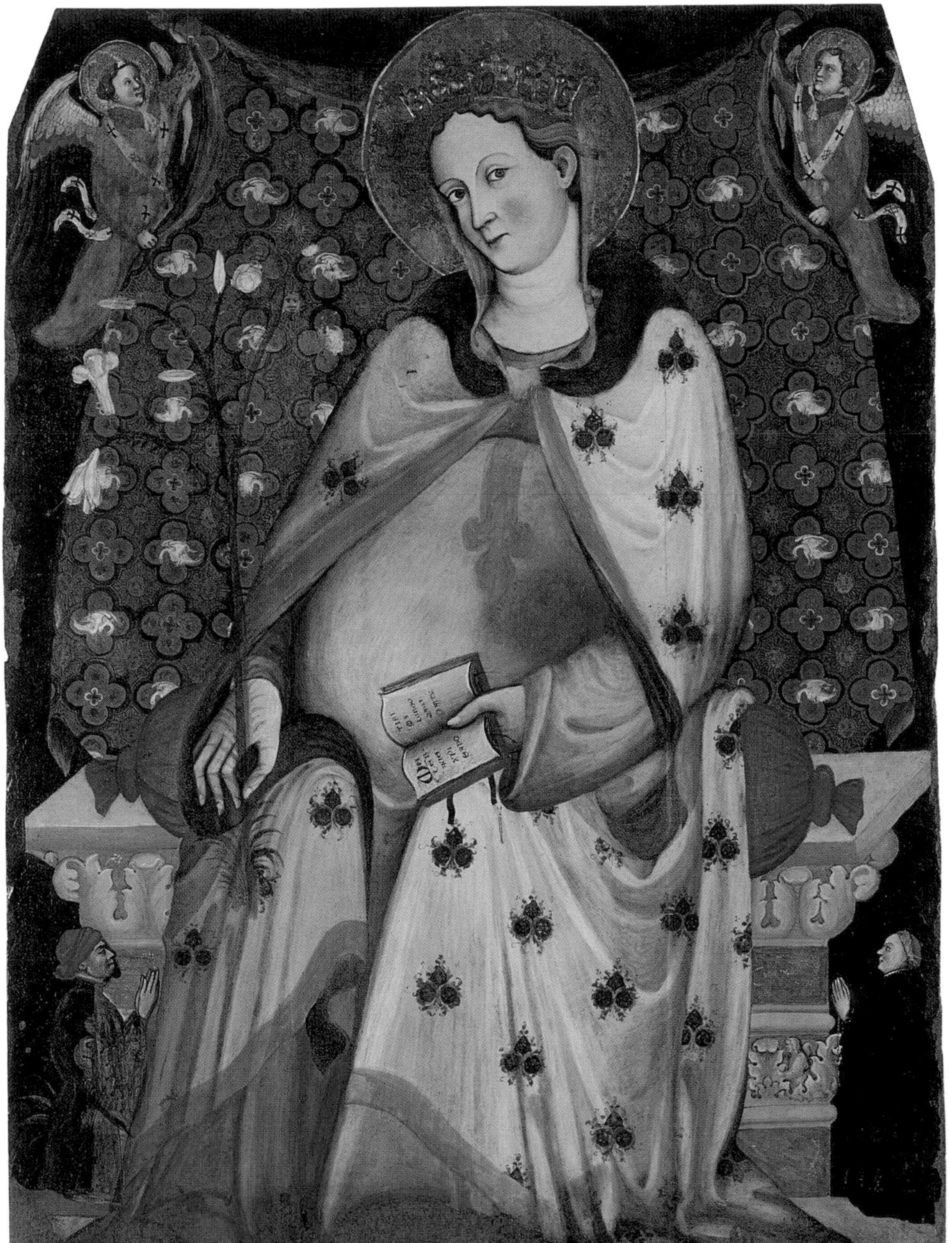

23

this register still exists in the Seminary. The ascension of Gabriele Condulmer from the order of the Lateran Canons to the papacy (Eugene IV) in 1431, and his long pontificate, which lasted until 1447, brought new-found glory and power to the monks of La Carità. In fact, after prolonged negotiations with the members of the Scuola di Santa Maria della Carità, the monks obtained approval to enlarge the church. The new construction began in April of 1441 and was overseen by Bartolomeo Bon. Working with his son, Giovanni, Bon was responsible for all the stone work that carried the new structure: the windows, the door with the lunette above it, the side door, the round eye which was once part of the façade, the statues of Saint Augustine, Saint Jerome and the Holy Father, the small bell-towers, the pinnacles, the leaves on the spire of the façade (most of which now lost), the side pillars, the ribs for the archivolts of the chapels, the cantilevers and every other decoration. At the same time, the walls were constructed in brick up to the roof, supported by fifteen beams of enormous dimensions from the region of Cadore, today still resting upon Bon's cantilevers which were completed in May of 1446, with the monogram "Ihesus". In 1450 the apse chapels were built and alongside Bartolomeo Bon we still find "Maestro Pantaleon", who appears to have been associated with Bon in many important workshops in Venice at that time, including the one at Ca' d'Oro.

The decoration painted with large leaves which runs under the scarp wall of the roof and surrounds the eye on all the windows was the work of Ercole, the son of Jacobello del Fiore. Once the construction was completed, the friars decorated it with precious works of art. In 1453 a Madonna was bought from Donatello, who was sojourning in Padua at the time; the painting was placed over the door of the sacristy. Other works were commissioned from Jacopo, Gentile and Giovanni Bellini and their studio and from Cima da Conegliano. Many important funereal monuments were also erected, such as the one for the doges Marco and Agostino Barbarigo. Parts of these statues remain today and are preserved in the Franchetti Gallery at Ca' d'Oro and in the Seminary. In 1807, the whole complex of the Carità – comprising the convent, church and school – was chosen to be the site of an Academy of Fine Arts and an accompanying gallery. Begun in 1811, the modifications were headed by the architect Giannantonio Selva. The church was completely overhauled: every decoration was removed, the "barco" (low porticoed wing) and the chapels were destroyed, the Gothic windows were walled over and the entire space was divided horizontally to create five large rooms on the upper floor, lighted by skylights for exhibiting. The bas relief work by Bartolomeo Bon on the façade showing the *Coronation of the Virgin* was removed, and is now preserved in the old sacristy of the church of the Salute.

From 1921 to 1923, under the direction of Gino Fogolari and with the architect Aldo Scolari, the whole space with the apses was restored including the truss ceiling and the Gothic windows on the side walls. In 1948 the room was remodelled by Carlo Scarpa.

Out of respect to the few original architectural features remaining, the arrangement took on the appearance of a provisional exhibition space. Today the room is largely kept free to provide space for temporary shows, although some important works are on permanent display along the walls.

The right apse chapel is periodically occupied by shows of works from the Accademia's collection in storage. At the end of the 19th Century the remains of glass frames from the second half of the 14th Century were placed on the windows of the central chapel; these frames once decorated the minor apses of the church of Santi Giovanni e Paolo.

In this room are shown works from the Venetian school of the end of the 15th Century, and works by Jacopo Bellini, Gentile Bellini, Giovanni Bellini, Alvise Vivarini, Nicolò di Pietro, Nicola di Maestro Antonio di Ancona, Bartolomeo Giolfino, Maestro della Madonna del Parto, Bartolomeo Vivarini, Carlo Crivelli, Vittore Belliniano, Giovanni Mansueti, Jacopo Palma il Vecchio and Paris Bordon.

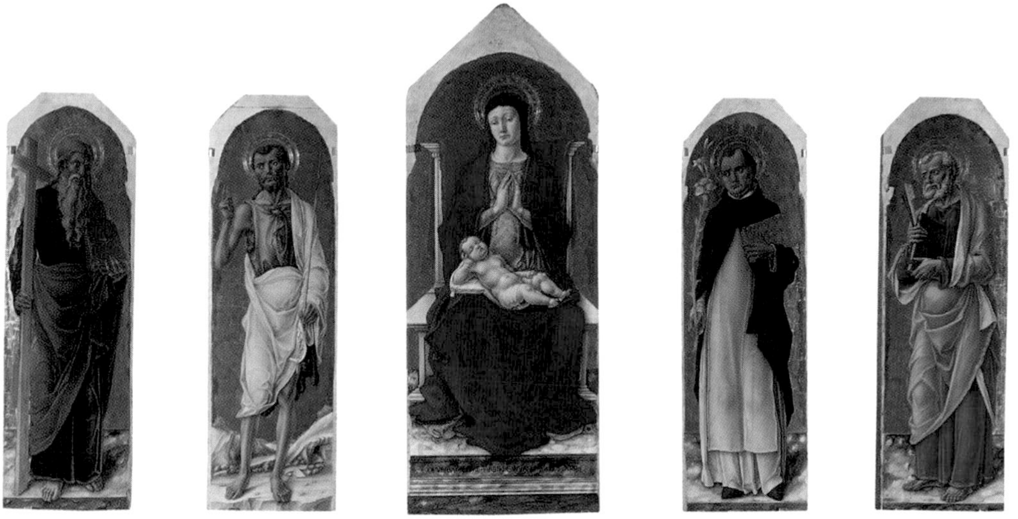

Bartolomeo Vivarini
(Venice c. 1430-records up until 1491)

Madonna Enthroned with saints Andrew, the Baptist, Dominic and Peter

Panels, gold background, cm 131 × 49, 107 × 33
(cat. 615)
Acquisition: 1812
Latest restoration: 1994

In the centre compartment toward the bottom is the signature and date of 1454. The polyptych comes from the church of S. Andrea on the island of Certosa, where it was placed at the altar of the Ca' Morosini chapel.

Alvise Vivarini
(Murano 1442/43-died between 1504 and November of 1505)

Madonna Enthroned with saints Ludwig of Toulouse, Antonio of Padua, Anne, Joachim, Francis and Bernard of Siena

Panel, cm 175 × 196
(cat. 607)
Acquisition: 1812
Latest restoration: 1993

On the base of the throne is the date 1480 and the signature. The work was originally on the altar of Santa Maria della Prà and then on the altar of San Bernardino in the church of San Francesco in Treviso.

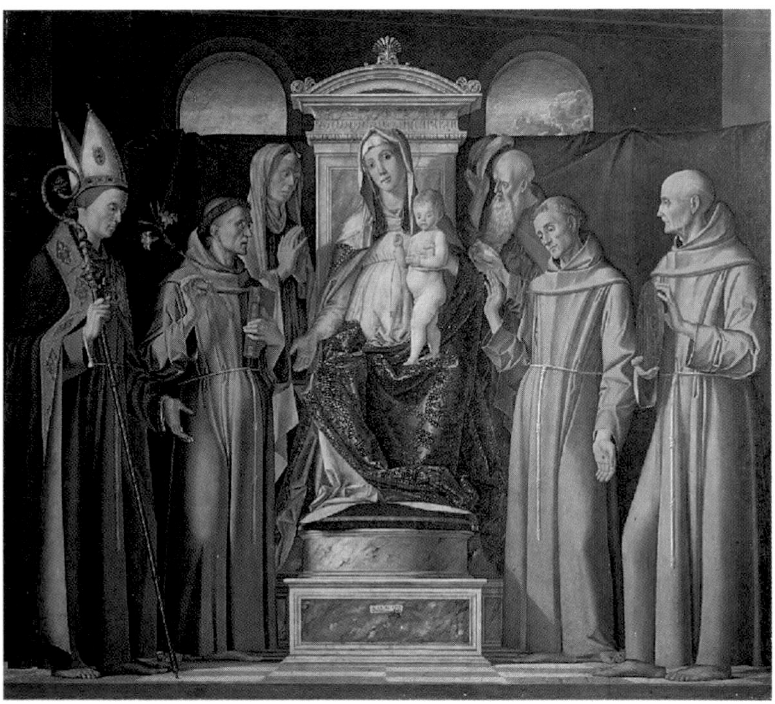

The apse triptychs. On the side walls of the apse are four triptychs that were originally in the Chiesa della Carità, on the altars of the noble chapels up against the "barco" (a structure similar to a chancel) erected between 1460 and 1464, while in 1471 all the altars were consecrated. Traditionally attributed to Vivarini, these triptychs were later brought back to Bellini, at Jacopo's studio, whose drawings are recorded with his first collaboration with Giovanni and Gentile, connecting them to the end of the sixth decade.
The archaic use of a gold background could be attributed to the use of assistants from Murano or to the wishes of the commissioners of the work. Nevertheless, the overall form of the works, with the lunettes above, borrowed from Mantegna's altarpiece for San Zeno in Verona, must have had a great impact on Venetian artistic culture.

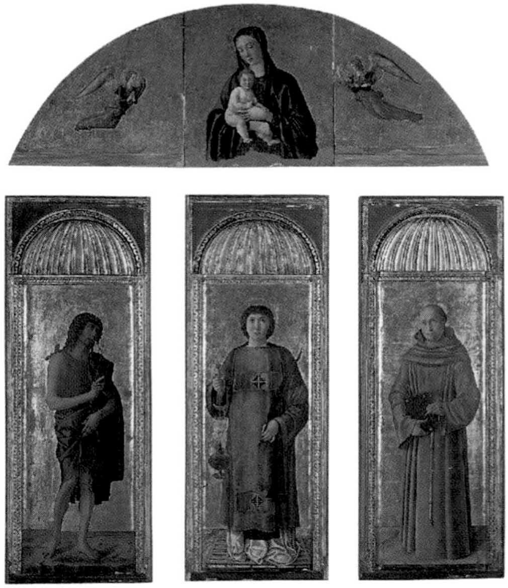

23

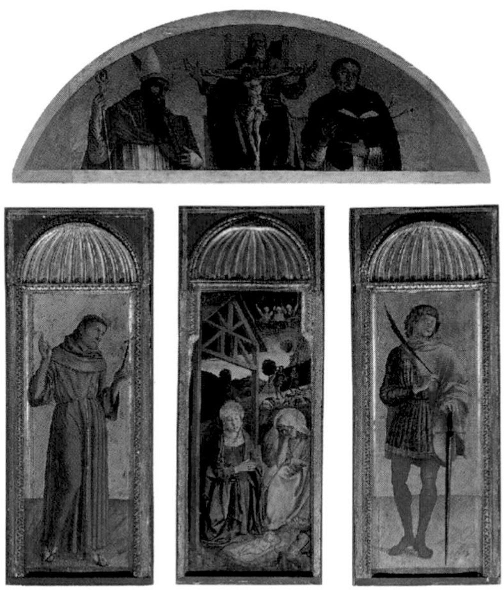

Jacopo Bellini, Gentile Bellini, Giovanni Bellini and collaborators

Saint Lawrence and the Madonna Polyptich

Panel, gold background cm 103 × 45 (Saints Lawrence and the Baptist), 127 × 48 (Saint Anthony), 57 × 188 (cm (the lunette, divided at the back into three parts) (cat. 621/B)
Acquisition: 1812 (Saints Lawrence and the Baptist), 1834 (Saint Anthony), 1923 (the Madonna), 1954 (the two angels)
Latest restoration: 1948-49

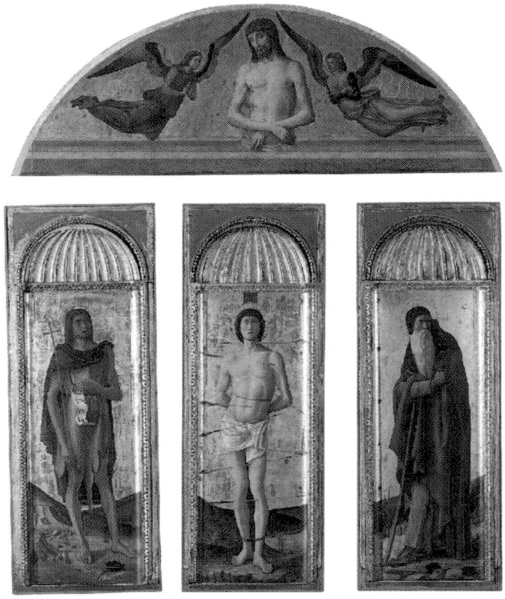

Jacopo Bellini, Gentile Bellini, Giovanni Bellini and collaborators

Saint Sebastian with Saints John the Baptist and Anthony Triptych

Panels, gold background, cm 103 × 45 (Saint Sebastian and Saint Anthony), 127 × 48 (cm (John the Baptist), 60 × 166 (lunette) (cat. 621/A)
Acquisition: 1821 (Saint Sebastian and Saint Anthony), 1834 (John the Baptist), 1927 (lunette)

Jacopo Bellini, Gentile Bellini, Giovanni Bellini and collaborators

Nativity and Saints Francis and Victor Triptych

Panels, gold background cm 103 × 45 (Nativity), 127 × 48 (Saints Francis and Victor), 60 × 166 (lunette) (cat. 621)
Acquisition: 1834 (the saints), 1891 (Nativity),1923 (the lunette)
Latest restoration: 1948-49

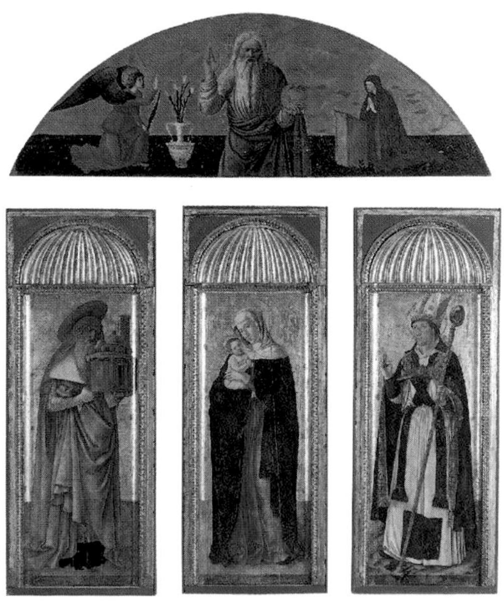

Jacopo Bellini, Gentile Bellini, Giovanni Bellini collaborators

Madonna with Child and Saints Jerome and Ludovic Triptych

Panels, with gold background, cm 127 × 48 (each) 59 × 170 (lunette) (cat. 621/C)
Acquisition: 1834 (Madonna and Saints), 1919 (lunette)
Latest restoration: 1948-49

23

Canvases from the Albergo Room of the Scuola Grande di San Marco. The five canvases located at the back of the church, together with the *Sermon of Saint Mark at Alexandria* by Gentile Bellini and the *Baptism of Saint Mark* by Giovanni Mansueti – today in the Brera Museum – were part of the original decoration of the Albergo Room of the Scuola di San Marco. In 1492 Gentile and Giovanni Bellini offered to paint the room, and came to an agreement with the Scuola. However, Gentile died in 1507 without finishing the Sermon, which was completed by Giovanni. In 1515 the Scuola hired Giovanni to paint the *Martyrdom of Saint Mark*, but unfortunately on November 29, 1516, the artist died and the work was left unfinished until Vittore Belliniano completed it in 1526. Later works were commissioned from Giovanni Mansueti, collaborator and disciple of Gentile Bellini, thus guaranteeing the stylistic continuity of the cycle. Mansueti died in 1526 or 1527, and the last two paintings, *The Presentation of Saint Mark's Ring* by Paris Bordon, and the *Sea Storm* by Palma il Vecchio, reveal a radical change in the taste of the commissioners. When the Scuola was suppressed by Napoleonic decree in 1806, the cycle was dispersed, with pieces in Milan, Venice and Vienna. The works in Vienna were returned in 1919 and the cycle was re-assembled and placed on display in the Galleries, but without the paintings in the Brera Museum, in 1994.

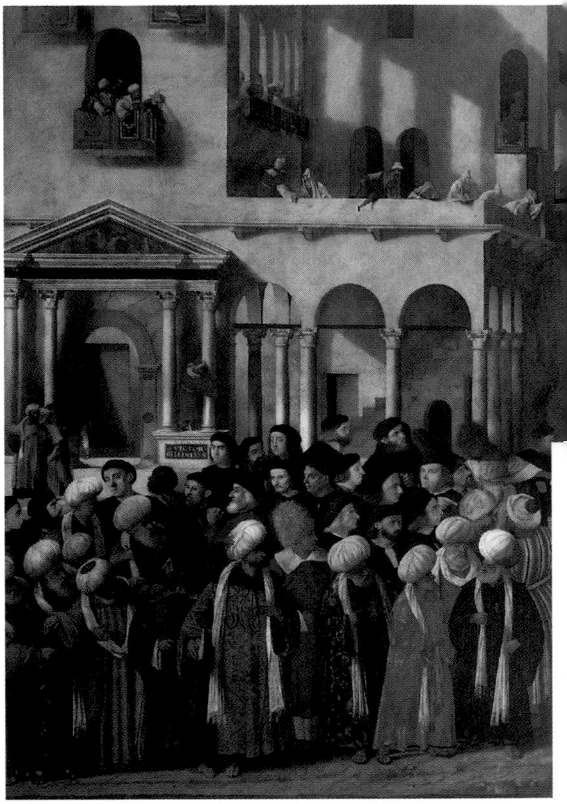

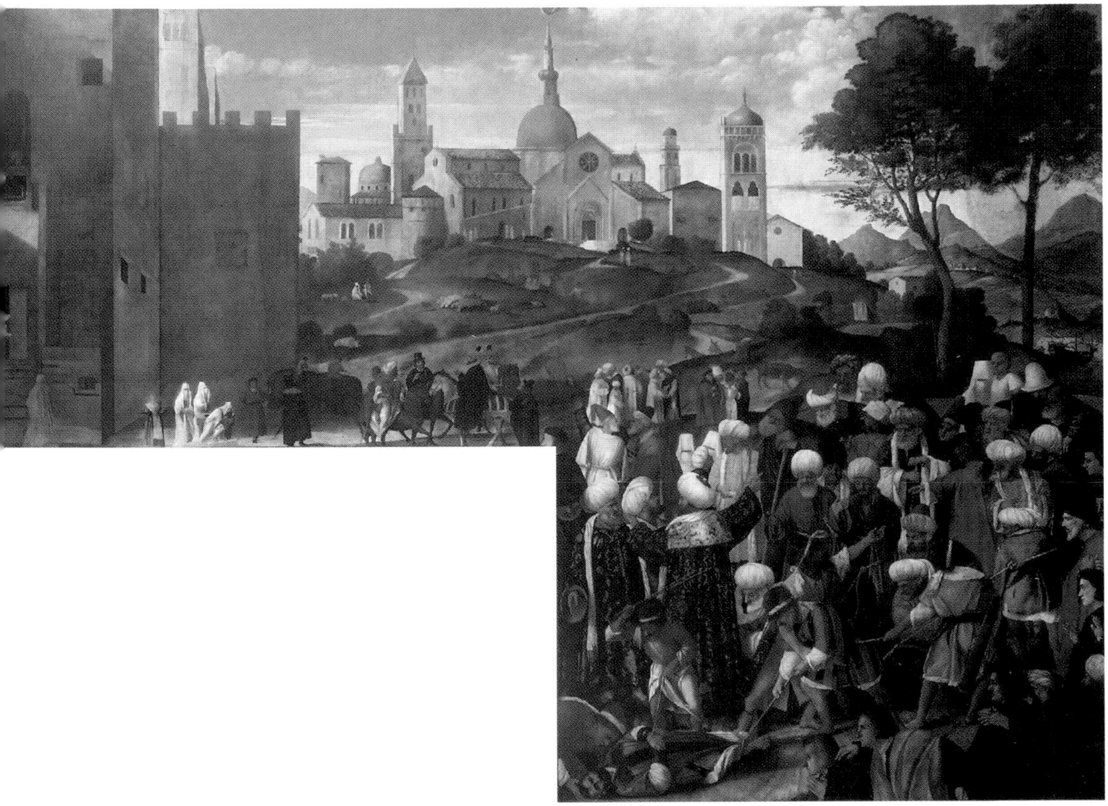

Giovanni Bellini
(1434/39-1516)
and
Vittore Belliniano
(records from 1507 to 1529)

Martyrdom of Saint Mark

Canvas, cm 362 × 771
(cat. 1002)
Acquisition: 1919
Latest restoration: 1987-94

On July 4th, 1515, the Scuola commissioned Giovanni Bellini to paint a canvas with the story of Saint Mark, who "... in Alexandria was dragged along the ground by those infidel Moors". When Giovanni died in 1516, the work was completed by Vittore Belliniano who placed his signature on it and the date of 1526 – ten years later. The drawing and layout of the great canvas are doubtless the work of Giovanni, but the actual painting of the canvas was by Vittore.

Jacopo Palma il Vecchio (Serina, Bergamo, c. 1480-Venice 1528) and **Paris Bordone** (Treviso 1500-Venice 1571)

Sea Storm

Canvas, cm 362 × 408
(cat. 516)
Acquisition: 1829
Latest restoration: 1993-94

This work depicts the legend of a fisherman saved from a storm by saints Mark, George and Nicholas. The work was probably commissioned immediately prior to the death of Palma in 1528, and so he may not have had the time to finish the canvas, which was completed or repaired by Paris Bordon in 1534.

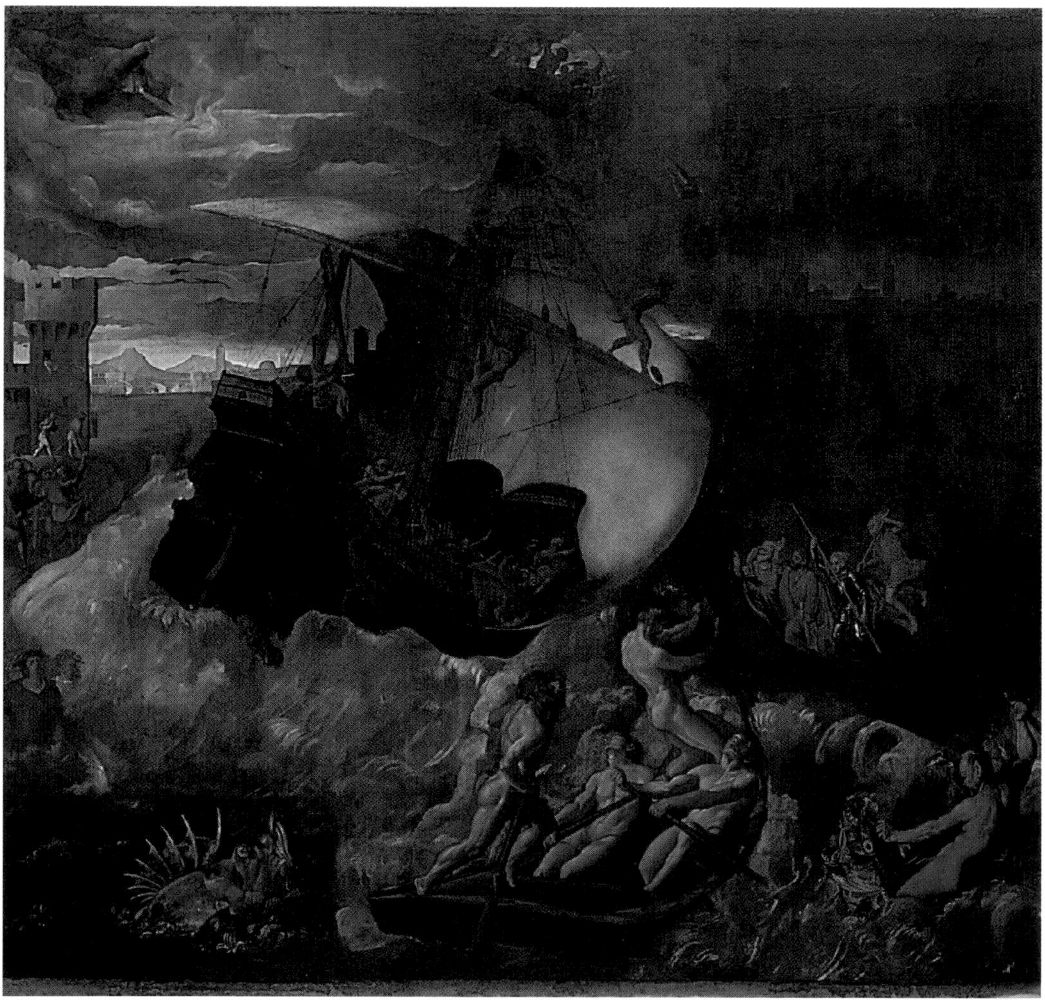

23

Paris Bordone
(Treviso 1500-Venice 1571)

Presentation of Saint Mark's Ring

Canvas, cm 370 × 300 (cat. 320)
Acquisition: 1815
Latest restoration: 1988

On the base of the pillar at right is the signature. The work shows the fisherman who offers the ring of Saint Mark to the doge as proof of the miraculous events of the night before. Surrounding doge Andrea Gritti (1522-1538) are the senators, while on the left is the great guardian and a group of members of the confraternity.
The execution of the canvas was decided in 1534, but it was probably painted around the first half of the 1550's.

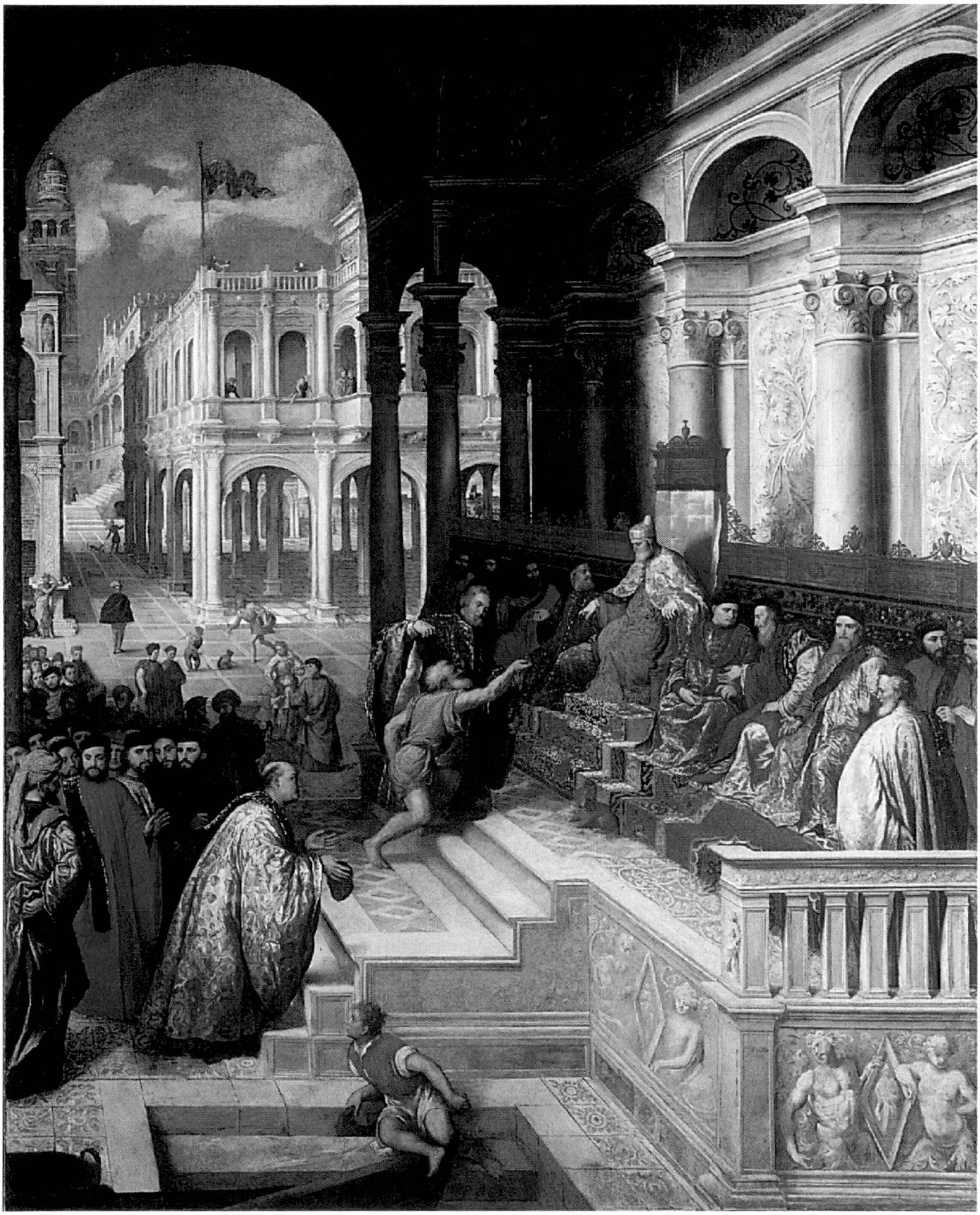

23

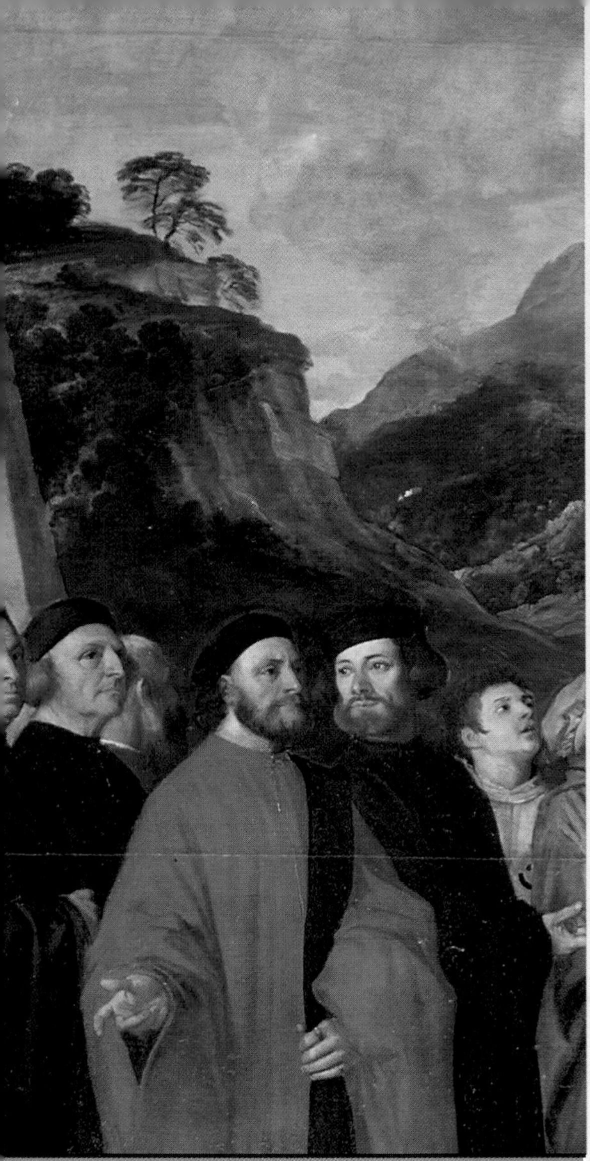

Former Albergo Room of the Scuola di Santa Maria della Carità. Titian, Antonio Vivarini and Giovanni d'Alemagna

This was the Albergo Room of the Scuola di Santa Maria della Carità, where the most highly ranked members met, and where the registers, charters (called the "mariegola"), and the relics were all kept. The ceiling, gilt and multicoloured, with the four *Evangelists*, dates from the end of the 15th Century. The *Holy Father* at the centre was probably taken from a previous ceiling in the Assembly Hall which may have been destroyed by fire. In 1811 Selva opened the short stairway; for this occasion the wooden altar was disassembled and the triptych by Antonio Vivarini and Giovanni d'Alemagna was moved to the right wall.
In this room are shown works by Antonio Vivarini and Giovanni d'Alemagna, Titian, the Veneto-Byzantine school of the 14th and 15th Centuries, an anonymous artist of the 16th Century and the Venetian school of the 16th Century.

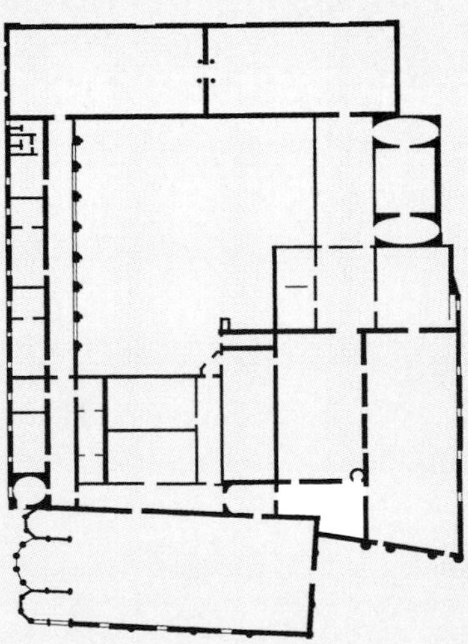

Antonio Vivarini
(1418/20 ca.-1476/84)
and
Giovanni d'Alemagna
(records from 1441-1450)

Madonna Enthroned with Saints Gregory, Jerome, Ambrose and Augustine

Canvases, cm 344 × 203 (central), 344 × 137 (sides) (cat. 625)
Acquisition: 1807
Latest restoration: 1999

On the step of the throne is written the date 1446 and the signature. One of the oldest Venetian paintings on canvas, it is certainly the most unified work the two artists produced in their problematic collaboration. The Virgin and angels are clearly attributable to Vivarini.

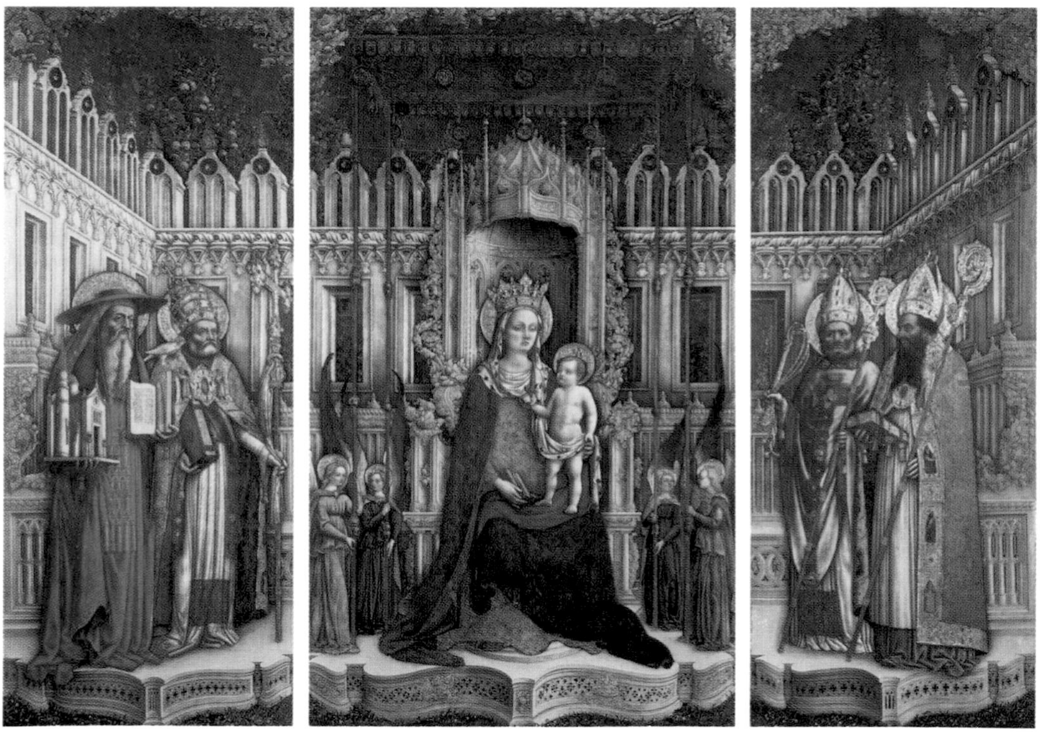

24

Titian
(Pieve di Cadore c. 1480/90-Venice 1576)
Presentation of the Virgin
Canvas, cm 335 × 775 (cat. 626)
Acquisition: 1807
Latest restoration: 1981

This large canvas was painted for the Albergo Room of the Scuola della Carità between August 21, 1534 and March 6, 1539. It appears to have been cut below to accommodate a door. If the horizontal path of the wall has imposed a certain design taken from the Venetian narrative tradition – and mostly from Carpaccio – it does so with an extraordinarily "modern" spirit and a deep awareness of the contemporary architectural notions proposed by Sansovino and Serlio. The perfect balance between architecture and landscape, and of both with the open procession of the members of the confraternity, firmly establishes the unity of the work.

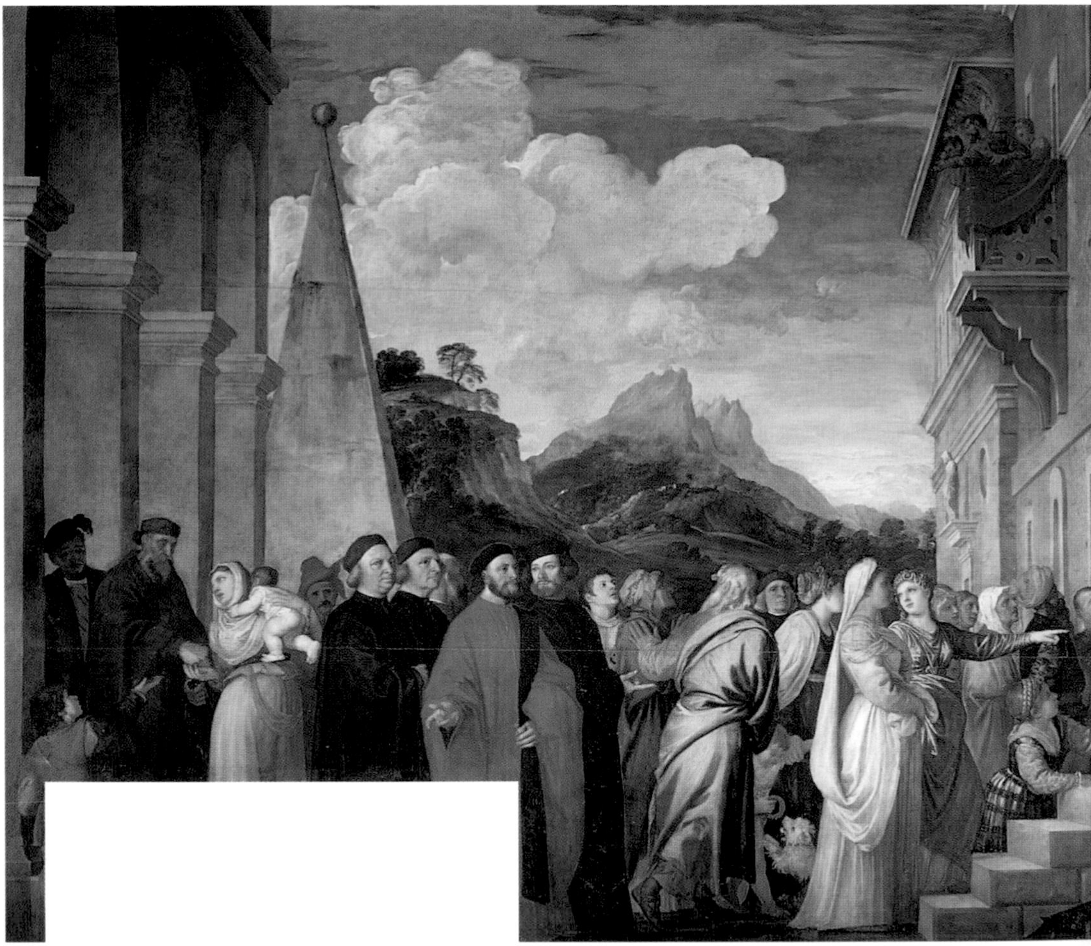

24

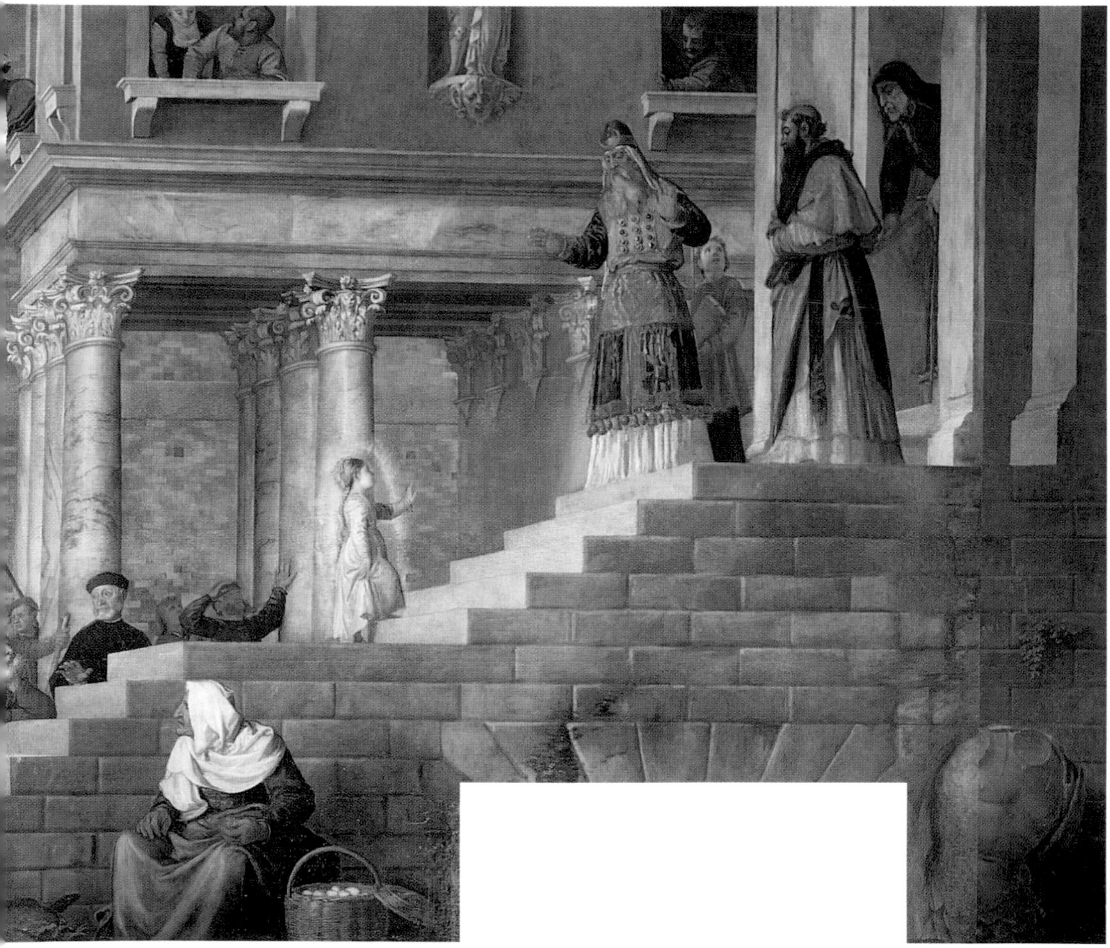

24

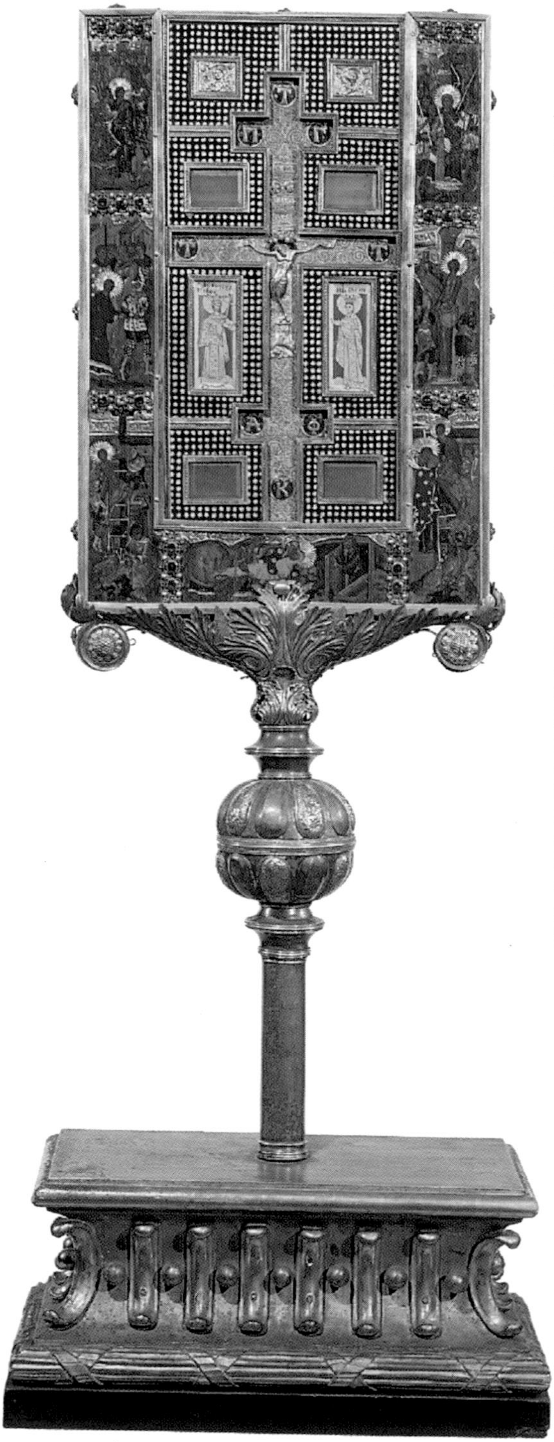

24

Veneto-Byzantine School of the 14th and 15th Centuries

Reliquary of Cardinal Bessarion

Wood, silver, gilt filigree, enamel, glass and precious stones, cm 47 × 32 (cat. 519)
Acquisition: 1919
Donated to the Scuola della Carità in 1463 by Cardinal Bessarion.

The precious piece is formed of a cross with Christ encased on an enameled tablet which includes four rock crystal cases containing the "Holy Wood" and "Holy Shroud" relics, two plates with the archangels Gabriel and Michael, Constantine and Saint Helen painted on glass, a cover composed of a fixed part framing the reliquary on three sides with seven small scenes from The Passion and a moveable shutter cover on which the Crucifixion is depicted.

Printed by Elemond S.p.A. in Martellago Mondadori Printing S.p.a.
via Castellana, 98 - Martellago (VE) in the year 2000